PRESIDENT DONALD TRUMP
THE SHAWN MENDES CONSPIRACY

HOW OPERATION COVFEFE
SECURED THE WHITE HOUSE

COPYRIGHT

About the Author

Aside from having a deep hatred of onions, and apparently having an exceptionally high level of insight into the Trump Administration, Jackson spends his time writing. He currently lives in Perth and practiced as a lawyer for a short period, before realising that he would like to retain his soul.

Contact

www.jacksonbrownauthor.com

Facebook: @jacksonbrownauthor

Email: jacksonbrownwriter@gmail.com

Other Works

The Burnt Bride

Introduction

'Robert Pattinson should not take back Kristen Stewart. She cheated on him like a dog and will do it again - just watch. He can do much better!' - Donald Trump, 17 October 2012, Twitter.

Donald John Trump. The name is famous, as is the man himself. Barely an hour will go by where his name is not mentioned in the news.

Born, conveniently enough after the end of World War II, on 14 June 1946, the man's seventy years on this planet has been marred by controversy and marked by achievements.

Love him or hate him, no one can deny that he has reached the pinnacle of human power in the 21st Century. Not only is his net worth counted in the billions, he has also successfully secured the most coveted office in the world - that of the Presidency of the United States of America.

Aside from managing to claim the title as the 45th president of the world's most influential nation, he also created one of the world's most overrated television shows - *The Apprentice* - and has written several books that contain as much useful information as this one.

Yet some would claim that having immense wealth and power is not everything, if a person does not have family. President Trump has also succeeded in this area. Whilst the average American only will ever have 1.4 wives in their lifetime (the 0.4 is an average, and not reflective of those married to dwarves), President Trump has had three. Two of which were human. Additionally, President Trump has five children. And unlike Jesus Christ, he had two parents.

So what is behind President Trump's successes? For decades Americans have wanted to know the answer. Was it because he was simply born into wealth? Was it due to his keen business mind after he learnt economics at the University of Pennsylvania? Or was there a hidden factor, an adviser perhaps, who was involved in every single one of his achievements?

It will surprise many of his supporters and detractors that the answer has been glaringly obvious for so long. The reason for President Trump being the man he is today can be answered in just two words - Shawn Mendes.

By now, the average reader will be raising their eyebrows at this claim. After all, how could a nineteen year old pop sensation have influenced the career of a seventy year old juggernaut? Even more importantly, how could a Canadian ever influence an American?

This book will seek to expose the truth that President Trump and Shawn Mendes have sought to cover for so long, via their joint 'Operation Covfefe'.

In order to assist readers, each chapter will be generally split into two segments. The first will be facts known to the public, which will provide a reader with a keen insight into President Trump's life, as well as those who have played a part in the election. The second part will contain information which your correspondent (i.e. me) has exclusively uncovered and has not yet been revealed. These sections will be eerily similar to anything published by Rupert Murdoch but after all, facts should never get in the way of a good story.

Chapter One

The Makings of a Legend

'Part of the beauty of me is that I am very rich.'
- Donald Trump, 17 March 2011,
interview with ABC's Good Morning.

Shawn Mendes was not born until 1998, when President Trump was only fifty two. Naturally, baby Shawn Mendes was in no position to counsel and advise the powerful businessman. It was not until 2013 that Operation Covfefe commenced.

However, no story on President Trump would be complete without going back to the early years. After all, readers will not be able to understand why he turned to the pop singer without having a thorough knowledge of his upbringing.

Money breeds money and greatness creates greatness. It is a sad, but true, fact of life that being born into wealth will greatly increase a person's chance of having wealth themselves.

All of Trump's grandparents were born in Europe, with his father's parents from Germany and his mother's parents from Scotland.

It was Friedrich Trump, the German, who began the Trump fortune by operating restaurants and boarding lodgings in booming mining towns during the Gold Rush, after emigrating to the USA in 1885. Friedrich was clever - rather than mine the gold himself, he would take money from the prospective miners. Therefore, his fortune was not dependent on blind luck but rather savvy business sense.

At this stage, readers should note that Friedrich started part of his business in the Klondike region. Why is this important? The region is located in Canada, which will factor considerably in 1998...

In 1902, Friedrich married Elisabeth Christ, on the basis of love, but also for the likely reason that his future grandson could use Elisabeth's surname to court religious voters. They had a child, Frederick Trump.

It was not all smooth sailing - Friedrich's business successes were to be short lived. In 1918, he died from influenza, leaving Elisabeth a widow.

Frederick was only fifteen when his father died, but immediately went to work with his mother in real estate. Together, they launched a company called Elisabeth Trump and Son, which, in future years, would eventually become The Trump Organisation.

It is surprising that one of America's most well known companies has its origins in being launched by a powerful woman. Not to mention, a powerful woman launched the company during the early 1900s and was in charge of its operations at a time when women were frowned upon for driving a bus or continuing to work once they had a child.

Frederick expanded the real estate business into building and selling houses and apartments. Whilst continuing to build the family wealth with his mother, he met Mary Anne, a Scottish emigrant, in New York. Mary worked as a maid, Frederick, a wealthy businessman. Some things in life do not make sense, but America has always been a nation where class rankings are not overly prominent. In 1936 the two married.

Mary the maid may not have worked as a chef, but she had no problem with placing buns in the oven. From 1937 to 1948, she had four children.

The first was Maryanne born in 1937, the second Fred Junior in 1938, the third Elizabeth in 1942, the fourth Donald himself in 1946, and the last was Robert in 1948.

1946 was the year in which the future world order was established. World War II had ended the year previously, resulting in American influence spreading throughout western Europe, as the Soviets sought to counter the risk of American-ideals in the east. The United Nations had its first meeting in 1946 and the Nuremburg war trials were occurring for the surviving Nazi leaders. Hope was in the air, after so many years of death and despair. But so was fear. Americans were incredibly wary of the rise of communism and the Soviet threat appeared real. The victory of World War II quickly turned to dread about a possible red future.

It is almost ironic that Donald Trump was born into this climate, for over time he would develop his skills for exploiting fear and hope to a level unmatched by any of his peers.

Raised in Queens, Donald Trump was an independent child who struggled with authority figures, preferring to set his own course. His parents, exasperated at his disobedience, sent him to the New York Military Academy at the age of thirteen.

Military academies were set up in order to instil a level of obedience and patriotism into its students. However, the often-harsh methods utilised by these schools would result in the students becoming lonely type figures who would control their own destiny. If Donald Trump's parents were hoping he would graduate from the academy as a polite, submissive man, they were in for a rude shock.

Despite his continued autonomy, Donald Trump was eager to follow in his father's footsteps. When he left the academy in 1964, he enrolled in Fordham University where he stayed for two years before transferring to the University of Pennsylvania to study economics. At the time, the University of Pennsylvania offered a rare real-estate course that Donald Trump was eager to take. In 1968, he graduated with a Bachelor of Science degree, majoring in economics.

It was during this time the Vietnam War draft was occurring. Controversially, Trump was not enlisted in the army. This would later come back to haunt him during the presidential race, as it is often expected in America that candidates have had some form of military service.

So here we have Trump, at the age of twenty two, freshly graduated from university and heir to part of the Trump family fortune. What was going through this young man's head at the time? Was he concerned about being drafted into an unwinnable war? Was he ambitious about his family's future? Or was he waiting for a pop singing sensation to tap him on the shoulder with a plan?

The latter. Trump had no plan of his own. He needed an adviser to tell him what direction to go in. Because of this, he fell into his family's company, joining Elisabeth Trump and Sons.

Within three years, he was promoted to president of Elisabeth Trump and Sons, a remarkable achievement for a twenty five year old, less so for receiving the promotion as a birthday gift.

Trump's first act was to rename the company 'The Trump Organisation', and thus began the rise of the name Trump in American society.

His fame increasing, Donald Trump soon caught the attention of the Czech model Ivana Zelnickova. Ivana was attracted to the wealth, power and prestige of the man. Donald viewed Ivana as a powerful ally who would enhance his own appearance and reputation. After all, in New York social circles the powerful were regularly judged by whom their spouse was.

In 1977, the two married. Donald Trump was thirty years old at the time, Ivana was twenty seven. That same year, Donald Junior was born. It was Donald Trump's thought process at the time that if he named his son after him, it would make it more likely for his son to donate a kidney in the future if needed.

Ivanka was then born in 1981 and Eric in 1984. Neither of these children was lucky enough to be named after Donald Trump.

Despite having given him three children, Trump's interest in his wife started to wane. Whereas when he first met her she was glamorous and famous, over time her looks began to fade and she was no longer involved in modelling. Donald Trump felt as if he was married to an average woman.

This here is key to Covfefe - Trump has always been attracted to power and status. Once that disappears, his interest vanishes also. So it was only natural that when he met television personality Marla Maples, he would be instantly attracted to her.

Here was everything he longed for - a woman younger than him and who had status. In 1992, the two slept together.

Surprisingly, Ivana was shocked. How could a man cheat on her? Worse, how could anyone sleep with Trump? She herself had not done so in years. Divorce followed soon after.

Trump and Marla continued to sleep with each other, which resulted in Tiffany Trump entering the world from a place Trump had entered many times. Not wishing to cause a scandal, Trump and Marla married in 1993. This marriage was shorter than his first, ending in 1999.

From 1999 to 2005, Trump was an unmarried man. He was free to do as he wished, which worried him. He needed another status symbol. Another celebrity to combine with his own. However, the past two wives had been disappointments. They were of the opinion that a husband should never bring back prostitutes into their bed. These annoyances were too much for a successful businessman to handle.

So he did the only natural thing possible - he needed to create a celebrity he could marry. Someone who would not argue or talk to him when the cameras were off. Someone who would nod when he was talking and never question his cologne choice. So he flew to Japan in 2004 with a purpose - to commission a human-looking robot to act as his wife.

Thus, Robot T-Melania was designed for Donald Trump. On 22 January 2005, Trump married the robot. However, it is not well known that she is a machine. To this date, people are still speculating if Melania has a body-double. Nothing could be further from the truth. She is simply robotic.

Chapter Two

The Birth of an Evil Genius

'My fingers are long and beautiful, as, it has been well documented,
are various other parts of my body.'
- Donald Trump, 20 November 2016, Twitter.

The 8th August will go down in history as the darkest day on this planet. Is this because in 1898 on this day Corn Flakes were invented? Or because in 1914 Montenegro declared war on Germany? Or worse, because on this day in 1945 the USSR created the communist government in North Korea?

No. It is because in 1998, on 8th August Shawn Peter Raul Mendes was born. At this point, it would have been obvious to any keenly-eyed observer that the newly born baby was destined to act as an adviser to Donald Trump. Why?

There are few individuals on this planet who are named after Trump. But if you rearrange the letters found within Shawn's full name, you can create TRUMP.

Further, born in Toronto, Ontario, he was the son of a real estate agent mother and a businessman father. Note the key similarities here. Both Donald Trump and Shawn Mendes were born into families that engaged in real estate and business. From the moment they both came into this planet, they were exposed to similar themes. This would later lead to a close bond between the two men.

Shawn had a similar independent streak to Donald. However, the 1990s were different from the 1940s, as were parenting tactics.

Whereas previously military academies were the solution to hot-headed children, the 1990s saw the rise of the Internet and the 21st Century (in which Shawn spent the majority of his childhood) carried with it a number of amazing substitute parenting tools. Most notably, YouTube.

Shawn turned to YouTube in his early teen years and learnt many of the skills that would later come into great use. It was on this site that he managed to teach himself to play guitar by the age of the thirteen, without any tutors. The sense of achievement this gave Shawn no doubt drove him to learn other key skills on YouTube.

For example, there are a variety of YouTube videos that provide advanced learning on manipulation and American politics. Given Shawn's later hobbies, it is inconceivable to suggest that he did not spend hours watching and re-watching these specific videos.

The art of manipulation is a highly prodigious area, that only a few people can truly master. There are many subtle methods needed to be utilised by a true manipulator, and the average person is unable to utilise it effectively. Further, a certain level of charisma is needed by a manipulator. Charisma is best delivered by the position a person holds in society. For example, your local bus driver is less likely to be charismatic than your high level politician.

Realising this, Shawn Mendes knew that he needed to create a significant online profile to boost his charisma and, by extension, his manipulative skills.

In 2013, he decided to create a profile on the social media platform Vine. This platform, which now no longer exists for mysterious reasons, allows its users to upload short videos. Shawn Mendes used this to upload singing renditions of popular songs. Due to his talent, he quickly gained millions of followers on Vine within only a few months.

This by itself has caused many commentators to raise their eyebrows, although none dare ask the question. How did a fifteen year old schoolchild manage to create a following of over a million followers within two months? How did he achieve a loyal following that would regularly log in for the sole reason of seeing his videos?

In February 2013, he was beginning to get the attention of Washington insiders, who were keen to harness the power of social media, after seeing its influence in the 2012 presidential election. Barack

Obama's chief adviser noticed the power Mendes was beginning to generate and wanted to tap into this. However, as Shawn Mendes was a Canadian citizen, he was limited in his approach.

Enter Hillary Clinton, the Secretary of State, whose whole job was to deal with foreigners, including Canadians.

To explain what happened on 1 February 2013, your correspondent will use some poetic licence to provide a flashback of the dark events...

Hillary looked out at the snow covered street, as her limo sped down the road. She sighed to herself, thinking back to the mountain of paperwork awaiting her. There would be another work-filled weekend ahead of her. Not that this raised any great concern. Any weekend she could use to work instead of having to see Bill was a relief these days. Lately he had been very... persistent, in his efforts to get her to run for the presidency in the next election.

She was content with her position as Secretary of State, and had no intention of running. Having seen firsthand the stresses of the office on both her husband and Barack, she could not see why she would want to do it. Besides, having gone for the Democrat nomination once was enough. She did not feel she had the energy to do it again. Even though there was some small part of her that still longed for it, she could not see it happening.

No, when she finally returned home she would tell Bill that she was not going to run. She would see out her term as Secretary of State and then quietly retire, never again seeking the limelight.

'Ma'am, we are five minutes away,' the driver's voice said over the intercom.

'Thank you,' she said, without turning away from looking out at the Toronto street. She felt almost naked in Canada, having been forced to leave her security behind. No one could know about this, Barack had said. Instructing her to only take her most loyal staffer as a driver, she was to tell all others she was simply attending to the Libyan issues.

Hillary understood the need for secrecy in this matter. After all, she only created her second private email account so she and Barack could communicate on this mission in private. The press must not be allowed to discover their plan. If the Republicans even got a whiff of what she was doing...

The limo pulled to a stop, outside a double storey home. With the garden well kept, and the surrounding houses similarly designed, Hillary got the distinct impression of an American-style street.

'Perfect,' she said to herself, feeling more at ease.

Patting down her pant suit one last time, she stepped out of the vehicle, not waiting for the driver to open the door. She waved back dismissively to him, to avoid him exiting. She trusted him with her life. But she would not trust him with this.

Her phone vibrated in her jacket pocket. Continuing to walk towards the front door, she pulled it out and glanced at the message.

"Hillary - thoughts on Jon Snow?" - John McCain.

She switched her phone off, not bothering to reply. There would be time later to speculate on the show's ending with the Vice President.

Before she could even knock on the door, it opened, revealing a young man looking out towards her, dressed in jeans and a grey shirt.

'Come in,' he said, moving aside.

'Thank you,' she said, inwardly grimacing at the slight tremor in her voice.

He led her towards the front lounge room and sat down on the solitary armchair. She sat on the opposite couch, smiling slightly at him whilst scanning the room. There were no framed photographs. It was almost as if somebody had stripped the room before she arrived, to remove any evidence.

'Are your parents home?' she asked.

'No,' he replied simply.

'Oh,' she said, resisting the urge to frown. She would need his parents to sign the consent form, if he agreed to be utilised.

'How are the talks going with Iran?' he asked.

'Progressing steadily,' she said, impressed that a fourteen year old would keep up to date with world events. 'We hope to secure real success shortly. It is difficult, but provided we continue to persevere I am sure that we can obtain results.'

'Some American voters will not want a deal done,' he said. 'You could lose some key support in the south.'

'Perhaps. But that is not our primary concern.'

'Shouldn't it be?'

'Why?' she said, puzzled. This conversation had not started how she anticipated at all. She had researched facts on Justin Bieber beforehand, believing him to be one of Shawn's idols.

'You will be running for the Democrat nomination in 2016, correct?'

'Presently I am fully committed to my role as Secretary of State in the Obama administration,' she said, reciting the one-liner her advisers had drilled into her.

He smiled, 'Yes, but 2016 is not presently. Are you not planning on running?'

'No,' she said. There was a plan in place for Barack's successor. A person waiting in the wings they all knew would succeed and make a fine president. Her dream had long died.

'Then what are you doing here exactly?'

'Oh,' she said, noticing they had completely dispensed with the pleasantries. 'I am here to offer you a job.'

'I worked out as much.'

Hillary smiled at him. The fourteen year old did not appear to be affected by her power at all. Most were intimidated, especially when she donned her power suit. But here was a kid, completely at ease and dictating the terms of their conversation. No wonder he had become such a power on social media.

'You are successful on the Vine.'

'On Vine,' he corrected.

'Yes, on the Vine. Your following is impressive. Lately, we have hit some walls in getting our healthcare legislation approved. The public is not aware of all of the benefits. Barack wanted to utilise the benefits of social media to get the youth involved. If they support this in great numbers, well, Congress will see that and be more likely to become amenable to Barack's requests.'

'Makes sense. Barack's social media strategy is lacking.'

'Lacking?' she said, the smile dropping from her face.

'Yes. It is very stiff. Fake. People can tell that he does not manage the accounts himself. They want to see genuine posts. Real posts. Not crafted stuff just designed for political purposes.'

'But social media is an advertising platform that-'

'No. Social media is a way for people to connect,' he said. 'If you approach it the wrong way, you will never be successful on it.'

Hillary nodded slowly, 'Yes, I see. Well, that is exactly why I am here. We want your expertise on social media. You clearly know how to use it and how to secure loyal followings. Barack wishes to hire you as his chief social media adviser. This all needs to be incredibly discreet. The American public would not support Barack hiring a Canadian.'

He leant back on the couch, with an almost disappointed look on his face.

'You want me to come work for Barack as a social media adviser?'

'Yes.'

'Then I decline.'

'If it is a matter of monetary compensation-'

'It is not.'

Hillary frowned. She was not used to people saying no to her, aside from in the 2008 Democrat election.

'Forgive me, but why did you agree to see me then?'

'I assumed you came here for a different purpose.'

'Which was?'

'To ask me to be your adviser.'

She leant forward, sensing an opening, 'Well, if you wanted to be my social media adviser, we could pass on that advice to Barack.'

'Not a social media adviser. A presidential adviser.'

'I am not running for president.'

'Yet.'

'If I ever did change my mind, why would I want you to advise me on that?'

'Because I can get you to win.'

She knew what he was saying was rubbish, but the small part of her that still hoped to one day become the president rose up inside her.

'How?'

'The future of society is social media. You may not fully understand it, but you know this. I achieved millions of followers in a month. Imagine what I could do for you in three years time.'

'You could secure me the presidency?'

'Yes.'

'Just say I was interested, what would be next?'

'You need to distance yourself from Barack. He is poisonous. The public want change. You need to resign from his administration immediately.'

Whilst the above has had some artistic licence added to it, there can be no doubt that this occurred.

For those readers who are questioning whether Hillary Clinton and Shawn Mendes did meet on 1 February 2013, I simply ask you one question.

What day did Hillary Clinton resign from her position as Secretary of State?

Correct. 1 February 2013. The same day she and Shawn Mendes made a pact to join forces. But little did Hillary know, that she was being deceived.

Chapter Three

The Rise and Fall of Hillary Clinton

'The only card Hillary Clinton has is the woman's card. She's got nothing else to offer and frankly, if Hillary Clinton were a man, I don't think she'd get 5 percent of the vote. The only thing she's got going is the woman's card, and the beautiful thing is, women don't like her.'
- Donald Trump, 26 April 2016, Republican Victory Speech.

Christmas is a difficult time for most. Aside from the financial strain it places on many American families, the worst part about Christmas can sometimes be family itself. Forced into a social gathering with members of the family who you only see once a year, conversations are forced and smiles plastered on. Not to mention, there is always that one uncle who drinks far too much and gets frisky with the cousins.

But before you begin dreading the Christmas period, give some thought to the Clinton family. True, this family does not suffer through lack of money (although they will tell you otherwise in their numerous fundraising activities), but they are definitely not short on family dramas.

The Lewinsky scandal has become a running joke amongst the political elite, whilst half of voters are impressed by Hillary standing by her man, the other half criticise her for not divorcing him. Yet the fact that Bill Clinton slept with another woman did not result in the two splitting up. They maintained their so-called loving relationship for decades to follow.

After Hillary lost the 2016 presidential election, she wrote a book on what happened. Bill Clinton read the draft and suggested changes. Hillary decided to not incorporate the amendments. Since then, neither of the two has spoken and they now sleep in separate beds. What could have possibly been worse than Bill having sexual relations with that woman? What could have finally driven the nail into the coffin and broken these two apart?

In an exclusive, your correspondent can now reveal the exact amendments Bill Clinton wanted made. Hillary rejected these as she knew that the truth could not come out, or else their lives would be put in peril. Bill, a stalwart of truth and integrity, disagreed vehemently. This has resulted in the two suffering from an irrevocable tear in their relationship.

Before we get into the nitty gritty about what exactly went down, it will be helpful to summarise the known facts.

As most Americans would know, before the 2016 election the Trump and Clinton families were close. This relationship began in 2000, when the Clintons moved to New York to help Hillary begin her Senate push. As a wealthy family, the Clintons needed to ingratiate themselves with the elite of New York. This would serve two purposes. One, it would keep Bill distracted and out of other peoples' pants, and secondly, it would help with their future fundraising efforts.

Bill wanted to join a golf club, but after his image had been tarnished in the affair scandal, most golf clubs rejected him. This was a sour note for a former president.

During this period, Donald Trump himself was refashioning his own image in New York, following his near-risk with bankruptcy. This included boosting his personality on the show 'The Apprentice'. As previously mentioned, Trump was obsessed with celebrity. He wanted to make a name for himself and surround himself with others who were famous. This included the Clintons.

Noting that Bill Clinton had been rejected from various golf clubs, he developed his own golf club in New York that he opened in 2002 - the Trump National Golf Club. It was conveniently located only six miles from Bill's house. Immediately, Bill joined the club in 2002 and he and Trump played many rounds together. To this date, Bill Clinton still has a locker at the golf club and goes there to play regularly. This is interesting, given the apparent bitterness that existed between the two families during the election.

Trump became a big fan of Bill's. He viewed him as a kindred spirit, because both of them had suffered through negative press and had allegations thrown against them about their treatment of women. From 2002 to 2009, Trump would regularly donate funds to the Clinton Foundation to assist Hillary with her Senate elections.

Further of note, Trump would regularly switch his registration from the Democrats and Republicans, to keep people guessing about his affiliation.

The closeness of the relationship between the two families is highlighted when Hillary and Bill attended Trump's wedding to the machine Melania.

All of the above is fact and within the public knowledge. Despite the existence of a close relationship, neither Trump nor Hillary ever publicly commented on how, or whether, their friendship broke down. It seems astounding for Donald Trump to financially support Hillary to get into politics, but then to later call for her to be 'locked up'. Clearly, something was amiss.

When we last left Hillary, it was 2013. She was Secretary of State and had met with Shawn Mendes, in an attempt to hire him as a social media adviser to the President of the United States. Shawn rejected this offer, knowing the role was a minor one that would not enable him to influence policy or pull the strings behind closed doors. Instead, Shawn countered with an offer to become Hillary Clinton's chief adviser for the 2016 Democrat race. That day, Hillary resigned as Secretary of State, and thus began her not-so-secret run to lead the Democrats.

The key issue here is that Hillary did not consult with Bill on her resignation. She announced it and then called him to tell him what she had done. At the time, Bill was playing golf with Trump. When Trump heard that she had resigned, he reportedly smiled. His plan was working (more on this later).

Hillary Clinton is a highly intelligent woman who is capable of making her own decisions without the need to consult her husband. As a former lawyer and partner of a law firm, there can be no question as to her analytical skills and ability to weigh up the advantages and disadvantages of each decision. However, in most close relationships partners will consult with one another before making a life-changing decision.

Bill was highly offended at not being informed or kept in the loop of the decision. It was at this point in time that the cracks began to form in their relationship and would slowly build up before completely breaking in 2017.

Rumour has it that Bill was firmly against her decision to resign in 2013. Whilst he was eager for her to run for the presidency, as he believed this would continue his legacy, it was his belief that she would best be able to do so by remaining in the public light as Secretary of State for at least two more years. After all, the Democrat nomination process would not commence until February 2016. There was still a period of three years before she needed to run.

Hillary's public position was that she needed the three year period to distance herself from Barack Obama, who was becoming increasingly unpopular at the time, and to begin fundraising for her campaign. After all, presidential elections are not cheap.

Bill did not buy this argument. For one, she would be running for the Democrats. Distancing herself from the current Democrat President was pointless. She had been part of his administration. No matter what she did voters would view them as one. And if she tried to distance herself too much, she would be tainted with allegations of disloyalty. As for the funds, Bill himself was a former president and could easily fundraise on her behalf. Not to mention, at this stage Donald Trump was still a key ally of the Clintons and Bill expected Trump to assist financially with any future campaign. Bill had no idea of Trump's own inclinations.

Bill knew that something was amiss. Despite their past differences, Hillary had always come to him for political advice. During her senate career and later executive career as Secretary of State, Bill was viewed as her closet adviser and confidante, along with their daughter, Chelsea Clinton. To suddenly not seek his advice, on a matter on which he was an expert, made Bill extremely suspicious.

The lives and thought processes of politicians are very different from the average American. Whereas most men would suspect that their wives were being unfaithful, Bill suspected that Hillary had hired a new adviser. And so she had.

Details of their arrangement were hammered out from 1 February 2013 until the 10 February 2013, when Shawn Mendes unofficially became the Chief Adviser to Hillary Clinton. This arrangement would only last until October of that year, when he was unceremoniously dumped from the position.

It is easy to see the logic of Hillary Clinton in appointing Shawn Mendes. Hillary was born in 1947, one year after Donald Trump. This made her, to speak crassly, quite old by 2013 in comparison to Barack Obama, who was fourteen years her junior (ironically enough, Shawn Mendes was fourteen in 2013). Whilst she had certain attributes necessary to success - high intelligence, strong leadership abilities and a perfect figure for a pants suit - she was unable to connect properly to voters.

Most viewed her as wooden and a career politician. Her public statements had the certain fake-edge to it that most long-term diplomats suffer from. She was unable to be herself in public and, in the rare moments where she did let her guard down, it had an almost 'lame'-like quality to it.

With the 2016 election shaping up to be the first election without an awe-inspiring candidate, Hillary knew that there would be a low turn-out unless a candidate did something to grab the attention of the nation. There would be no 'Yes We Can' campaigns with the first black candidate running, promising to make sweeping changes. Instead, there would be a bunch of politicians running for politics, an idea that sent the most switched on observer to sleep.

Shawn Mendes offered her the solution. With his ability to amass huge followings on social media, Hillary could tap into the youth vote and other demographics that she had previously failed to inspire. Once the following had been obtained, she could then galvanise them online and get them out to voting booths on election day. In most elections, candidates spend the majority of their time motivating people to take the effort of going to vote, as voting is not compulsory in the USA. If this could instead be achieved on social media, Hillary would be able to spend her time doing other things, such as buying more pant suits.

It was in March 2013 that Hillary Clinton formally set up her Facebook account and hired a team of university graduates to manage her page, under the watchful eye of 'Peter March', the pseudonym Shawn Mendes went under so none of the graduates would realise the truth. This was the start of her Democrat social media dominance. No other candidate during the 2016 nomination managed to match her presence on social media or reach. Even Bernie Sanders, who was viewed as a revolutionary candidate for the Democrats, was unable to get even half of the reach that Hillary enjoyed.

This frustrated her opponents greatly. They could not understand how a woman in her sixties could be beating them on social media. Many tried to uncover the secret of her success and many failed.

Because of her push on social media, the rise of Hillary Clinton in securing the Democrats nomination can be traced back to 2013, when Shawn Mendes was acting as her adviser. However, her fall in the presidential election can also be traced to October 2013, when she dismissed Shawn from her service.

From February until October, Shawn provided Hillary with some key advice. Aside from her growth on social media, this advice can be attributed to fundraising efforts, the formation of the Ready for Hillary political action committee, the proposed improvements on the *Affordable Care Act* and her policy of improving middle class incomes. On every single decision Hillary made during this time, she consulted with Shawn Mendes, to the exclusion of Bill.

Readers will now be wondering why Hillary decided to sack Shawn, if he was proving to be such an effective adviser. Well, this all goes back to Bill, who had become increasingly despondent throughout the year as he observed Hillary drawing further and further away from him.

Now, Bill Clinton may have the voice of a seedy white van owner and the sex libido of a Spanish teenager, but he is no idiot. Having been Governor of Arkansas for over nine years and President of the United States of America for eight years, he was well versed in conducting investigations. Or rather, hiring others to perform investigations for him.

After having watched the Sherlock Holmes films, Bill contacted Robert Downey Jr, hoping to enlist his services. Unbeknownst to Bill, fictional characters are not real and Robert politely declined.

So Bill went down a more appropriate avenue and hired a Lucas Johnson, who was a local New York private investigator, charging a standard three hundred dollars an hour. This was chump change to Bill and he happily signed the contract. What was Johnson's assignment? Discover who the adviser to Hillary Clinton is.

Lucas Johnson was forty years old in 2013. An ex New York cop who had been dismissed for taking bribes, he was a notorious alcoholic and always managed to pay his bills late. He thought his luck had changed when he received a call from Bill. All private investigators know that securing a contract with a leading politician was a win. They would always have dirt available to be dug up on their opponents, meaning that future work was secured.

For once in his life, Johnson put all of his effort into the investigation. However, Hillary was very skilled at hiding her tracks. She had a variety of different email accounts Johnson did not know about, so his attempts at infiltrating her digital communications revealed nothing at all.

At this point, no one in the US aside from teenage girls was aware of Shawn Mendes. Johnson could not have reasonably suspected that Shawn was Hillary's secret adviser, especially because the two rarely met in public. All he had to go on was Bill's suspicions.

Johnson was beginning to get worried by September 2013. He had now been engaged for over seven months but had turned up nothing for Bill, who was becoming frustrated with the lack of results. Bill reportedly told Johnson that if he did not find anything by the end of the month, his contract would be terminated and a new investigator would be hired.

With nothing to show for his months of effort, Johnson believed the writing was on the wall. He had hacked into Hillary's main email account to no avail, he had followed her comings and goings in New

York, and he had even set up a camera outside her New York house. Nothing was working.

In a last ditch attempt, he decided to spend a few days following her activities on social media, namely on Facebook and Twitter. Sipping coffee after coffee, he watched her every move, no matter how dull it was.

On 10 September 2013 Hillary followed seven pages that related to pant suits. On 11 September she poked Joe Biden on Facebook. And on 12 September 2013 she 'liked' a status Michelle Obama posted about the Obama dog.

On 13 September 2013 she followed Shawn Mendes on Twitter. Johnson was confused when he saw this. He did not know who this person was, and his search of US Congressmen and Senators came up with nothing. When he Googled the name, he found out that Shawn was a fifteen year old Canadian singer, who was beginning to amass a large following.

For ten minutes he stared at the screen, feeling like he had the pieces of the puzzle but not knowing how to connect it. Then it hit him. Here was a Canadian who knew about social media. And there was Hillary, following him on Twitter. Did it pass through his mind that maybe Hillary simply liked his music? No, Bill had told Johnson that Hillary only ever listened to classical music and heavy rock, never pop music.

Instantly, Johnson knew that he had discovered the identity of Hillary's secret adviser. However, Johnson did not go straight to Bill with the news. He was a dodgy ex-cop always looking to make more money. Instead, he went to Hillary to tell her what he had discovered.

When he confronted her at her New York home, she was shocked that somebody had uncovered the truth. She immediately went into damage control and agreed to pay Johnson the sum of one million dollars if he kept quiet. Hillary could not pay this amount without Bill finding out, so she put a call through to a wealthy family friend to arrange payment. Yes, Donald Trump paid off Johnson for Hillary Clinton.

One condition of Trump paying the amount was Hillary needed to fire Shawn from her service. Trump told her it was too risky to keep him on the books now that her secret had been discovered. Hillary agreed, despite her reservations that Shawn was a valuable adviser and losing him could potentially jeopardise her campaign.

A month afterwards, she sent Shawn an email via one of her secondary email accounts to tell him the news. They have never communicated since.

And what happened to Lucas Johnson? On Halloween of 2013, he was found dead in his apartment. Police ruled it as a suicide.

Some readers may speculate that Hillary had him killed, to hide what she had done. Others may think Shawn was behind it, as revenge. Those readers would be right.

Chapter Four

The Russian Influence

'Russia, if you're listening,
I hope you're able to find the 30,000 Hillary Clinton emails that are
missing. I think you will probably be rewarded mightily by our press.'
- Donald Trump, 27 July 2016, Press Conference.

The Russian Federation is the world's largest country in the world in regards to land mass and has the ninth largest population. Filled with a rich history and culture, the country has always had the potential to become one of the world's leading influencers and ideal tourist spot. Unfortunately, it has always been held back by its policies of invading neighbouring countries and conducting state-wide purges of any undesirables. This puts a damper on festivities.

Here we introduce the third world leader to this story, Russian President Vladimir Putin. Unlike Hillary and Donald, Vladimir was allegedly born in the 1950s. Prior to becoming President of the Russian Federation, he studied law at university and then worked as a KGB foreign intelligence officer during the era of the Soviet Union. Nowadays, he spends his time governing Russia and riding on horses shirtless. Since becoming President, his wealth has grown and he is now considerably worth more than Donald Trump himself.

Notably, in 2015 Pope Francis awarded Putin with the Angel of Peace Medal. Ironic, given the number of invasions Putin has overseen. On the other hand, this award is bestowed to any world leader that visits the Vatican.

There are some conspiracy theorists out there who believe Vladimir Putin is a vampire. They base this not on his looks or name, which both provide real evidence that he is a vampire, but on the fact that his appearance has not changed in the past one hundred years. Bizarrely, photos of Vladimir Putin exist before he was even allegedly born.

Whether Vladimir is a vampire or not is beyond the scope of this book. Nor is it relevant to the conspiracy that exists between Donald Trump and Shawn Mendes. This point is only noted out of interest to the supporters of Vladimir Putin, who may be surprised to find out that his diet only includes human blood and no vodka.

His immortal status notwithstanding, Vladimir Putin had a serious impact on the 2016 US election. Since the election, many Americans have wondered as to the extent of the Russian influence and there is presently a congressional investigation into the same. Special Counsel has been appointed and even the tech giant Facebook itself has been thrown into the fray, revealing that they have uncovered Russia purchased advertising that influenced the campaign.

Here is what is known as the facts so far…

Jeff Sessions, Trump's Attorney General in his Cabinet, met twice during the election with Sergey Kislyak, the Russian Ambassador to the US.

Rex Tillerson, Trump's Secretary of State, is the former CEO of ExxonMobil and did business with two of Russia's energy giants.

Michael Flynn, Trump's former National Security Adviser, met with Sergey Kislyak, was paid by Russia's propaganda network and in 2013 met with Russia's military intelligence agency. He has since resigned for not disclosing these facts.

Paul Manafort, Trump's former campaign manager, was a former business partner of a Russian oligarch and currently acts as an adviser to the former president of Ukraine, who is a close political ally of Vladimir Putin.

The Trump Organisation has a private server connection with Alfa Bank, Russia's largest bank, for no apparent reason whatsoever.

Felix Sater, Trump's business associate, was found guilty of stock fraud with Russian mafia figures.

Jared Kushner, Trump's son-in-law, also met with Sergey Kislyak during the election campaign.

As readers can clearly see, there are many links between the Trump administration and Russia. However, this by itself is not out of the ordinary. Trump is a leading businessman surrounded by key political and diplomatic figures. Russia is one of the world's leading nations. Clearly, the two will overlap in parts. What is an issue, however, is whether the Russians have involved themselves in the election to secure a more pro-Russian candidate in the White House.

In November 2013, a month after Hillary Clinton sacked Shawn Mendes, Donald Trump travelled to Russia. The public purpose of this visit was to host the Miss Universe Pageant. This was the first time in history that Russia had ever hosted a major beauty contest. The background to this event is bizarre.

Essentially, Emin Agalarov, the son of Russia's richest man (known as a Russian oligarch), released a music video featuring the 2012 winner of the pageant. This caught the attention of Trump who announced in June 2013 that the pageant would be held in Moscow later that year. Ten days later, Russia passed a series of anti-gay laws leading to controversy around the world. Trump maintained that the pageant would still be held in Russia regardless.

Trump then decided to issue one of his famous tweets where he wrote: 'Do you think Putin will be going to The Miss Universe Pageant in November in Moscow - if so, will he become my new best friend?'

It is not clear if Trump met with Putin during the pageant. However, in 2015 he was interviewed and asked about the pageant. He responded with:

> 'Two years ago, I was in Moscow. And a lot of the people, they were there, and they had an amazing time. And they're terrific people. You know, I was getting along with the oligarchs so great. I really loved my weekend, I called it my weekend in Moscow. But I was with the top level people, both oligarchs and generals, and top of the government people. I can't go further than that, but I will tell you that I met the top people, and the relationship was extraordinary.'

Three months after the pageant, Trump's daughter, Ivanka Trump, visited Moscow and was given a tour by none other than Emin Agalarov.

The closeness between the Trump family and leading Russian families was established in 2013. At no point in history had the US ever had a leader with such strong connections with their rival.

Yet all commentators are at a loss as to why Trump would decide on forging connections with Russian figures. Trump has minimal business interests in Russia. Rather, some of his key competitors are based there. There would be no direct financial incentive in setting up shop in Russia.

Could the reason have been to gain access to Russian hackers, to later secure information on Hillary? Again, this could not be the case. Every nation has hackers. And there would have been far less controversial and more discreet options out there for Trump.

Was it to gain support for his later presidential campaign? Perhaps, but why would he need Russia's support? They have never previously involved themselves in a US election and Trump himself is not short on funds.

Here was a wealthy man who already had enough money to fund his own campaign without going to Russia, to obtain an alliance that he did not need. Whilst investigations are currently continuing, no one knows the real purpose behind Trump's plan.

Until now.

It can be revealed that during the second part of Obama's presidency, Donald Trump had planted a junior staffer in his office, to report back to him on any developments. Using this staffer, Trump was able to stay one step ahead of Obama and foresee his every move.

In January 2013, Trump was informed that Obama wanted Hillary Clinton to approach Shawn Mendes to become a social media adviser. Trump knew this plan was doomed to fail, but suspected he may be able to poach Hillary's own adviser if he played his cards right.

On 28 January 2013, he anonymously sent a letter to Shawn Mendes, informing him that Hillary Clinton would later become a presidential candidate and that she would need him as an adviser. This was a cunning ploy on Trump's part. With one move, he would divide the Clinton and Obama camps, rendering them both weak. Further, he would implant ambition in the mind of Shawn Mendes, a celebrity he himself had watched and wanted to collect, just like he had with previous celebrities.

On 1 February 2013, when he was playing golf with Bill Clinton and Bill received a call from Hillary to inform him she had resigned, Trump knew that his plan was working.

He had achieved the impossible. Hillary Clinton would now run in the 2016 election, which worked in with his future plans. Recently, Obama had lost one of his highest performing Cabinet secretaries, which would result in his last years of presidency being filled with failures and non-results. This would make it easier for a Republican to win the 2016 election.

Trump knew that Shawn Mendes and Hillary Clinton would not work well together. Eventually, the relationship would sour and she would sack him or he would quit. When that time came, Trump wanted to be ready to swoop in and take on Shawn Mendes as an adviser himself. To do so, he needed to have a connection with Mendes.

Enter Island Records.

Island Records is a record label that represents a variety of musicians around the world. Some of their musicians include Bon Jovi, Fall Out Boy, Brian Fallon, Nick Jonas and The Weeknd. Whilst publicly a British company, it is secretly owned by Russian oligarchs that use it as a money laundering scheme. Through losses generated by Nick Jonas, Russian oligarchs get to funnel out their funds and avoid attracting the attention of the authorities.

Most relevantly, a subsidiary of Island Records represents Emin Agalarov, the Russian pop star who met both Donald Trump and Ivanka Trump. His father, being Russia's wealthiest man, ensured Emin's representation and success by funding his advertising.

9 November 2013, Moscow, Russian Federation

'Thank you for meeting with me privately, Aras,' Donald said, placing his small hand around the large whisky glass. 'And thank you even more for this whisky. This is the best whisky in the history of whiskies.'

'My pleasure,' rasped Aras, fighting back a cough. 'Russia thanks you for bringing this event, and the girls, to it.'

'Your son is an excellent host. The best host I have ever seen. No better. The best. He has a good future. Good man.'

'He does, as long as he remembers where his loyalty lies,' Aras said, pouring himself a glass of whisky. 'We always must look out for our children, must we not?'

'At times. But we are more important. If we do not look out for ourselves, who will?'

'Indeed, Mr Trump, indeed.'

'I came here for a specific purpose. You own Island Records.'

'The British own Island Records.'

'Yes, but all the same, you own it.'

Aras inclined his head slightly, 'You will find that I own nearly everything, be it partially or wholly. The world is indeed small.'

'I need you to sign up a singer.'

'A singer, you say.'

'Yes. A Canadian.'

Ares bristled slightly, 'A Canadian? That is some ask. Is he any good?'

'He has a few million followers on Vine. Not as many as I do, no. They love me on Vine. Really love me. They think I'm the best. But he does alright. He has a good voice. Not as good as my own, but a good voice.'

'And why do we want to sign him up? You have American owned record labels. Surely you have the influence to convince them to sign him?'

'I do. I definitely do. They love me too. But they would sign him up and make him their own. I need you to sign him up so I can later use him.'

'Use him? If it is those services you require-'

'Not like that. No. I love women. Women with big breasts. With bums I squeeze. Yes, I love women. That's why I run Miss Universe. I love women. And they love me. No, I want to use his influence for my own ends.'

'We can get that done for you, Mr Trump. However, when the time is right, we will call in this favour.'

In November 2013, a manager who worked for Island Records, Andrew Gertler, apparently discovered Shawn Mendes, conveniently two days after the above conversation.

By January 2014, Shawn Mendes was introduced to Island Records and officially signed in May 2014.

And so it began.

Chapter Five

A Music Career Built on Lies

'I'm just thinking to myself right now,
we should just cancel the election and just give it to Trump, right?'
- Donald Trump, 27 October 2016, Campaign Rally.

When Shawn Mendes signed the contract in May 2014 that would tie his musical career to Russian-owned Island Records, did the young man realise that Donald Trump was behind the deal? Did he know he was already being used by the property mogul to set him up for a future advisory position?

This is a difficult question to answer. By this point, Shawn was fifteen years old. He had taught himself how to play guitar, had accumulated a social media following of over four million, was a skilled singer, had learnt the subtle art of manipulation, and had acted as Hillary Clinton's adviser for eight months. This was a remarkable resume for both a young person and a Canadian.

Close confidantes of Shawn Mendes have reported he was shaken up after being sacked by Hillary Clinton. He had expected Hillary to win the 2016 election and was looking forward to calling the shots from behind the scenes. Rumour had it that he was considering running in the 2020 election, after Hillary's first term was up. The loss of his position hit him hard and made him re-evaluate his life's priorities.

When Russian plant Andrew Gertler approached Shawn, it would have been a lifeline to the despondent singer. After losing a key position with Hillary, here was now his chance to become a pop sensation.

Given his state of mind at the time, it is likely Shawn did not know that Donald Trump was behind Island Records. In any event, it was logical that a company would wish to sign up the popular singer, given his following.

In June of that year, Shawn released his first single. The song was called '*Life of the Party*' and achieved a top 25 ranking. Allegedly, Donald Trump wanted the song to be called '*Life of the Republican Party*' but Island Records resisted, informing Trump that this would reveal their relationship. Trump relented accordingly.

On 14 April 2015, Shawn released an album, with his chart-topping song '*Stitches*'. Again, the song title had a reference to Trump's affiliation with Island Records. In April 2015, Trump had his appendix removed. The stitches were a reference to the operation.

Later that year, he released a song called '*I Know What You Did Last Summer*'. This time, the song was a pointed attack towards none other than Hillary Clinton. Trump had discovered, using his connections in Obama's office, that Hillary Clinton had slept with Joe Biden in 2014, in an attempt to get revenge at Bill Clinton for sleeping with Monica Lewinsky. Trump wanted to send a signal to Hillary that he knew what she was up to.

Did Hillary know this was pointed at her? Possibly. She did, after all, have a history with Shawn Mendes and was likely watching his every move to ensure he did not go public. When she heard this song title, she may have suspected that he was targeting her.

In June 2016, Shawn released a new song called '*Treat You Better*'. In August, he released '*Mercy*'. It is believed the titles of these songs were aimed at detractors of Donald Trump, imploring them to treat Trump better and to have mercy on him.

Most recently, in April 2017 Shawn's released song was called '*There's Nothing Holdin' Me Back*'. This is in reference to Trump's ascension to President of the United States. There was, indeed, nothing holding Trump back from taking the top job.

This impressive musical career notwithstanding, at what point did Donald Trump approach Shawn to become his adviser?

It will surprise most readers that Trump did not do this until November 2015. This is almost a year and a half after he got Island Records to sign Shawn up. Further, it was five months after Trump announced his candidacy for President.

However, for those readers startled by this, a review of the key facts will make the issue clearer.

For a moment, please turn your minds to Shawn's early career. He was only signed to his record company in May 2014. Whilst he already had a following of over a few million on social media, at this point he did not have any original work to his name and was relatively unknown in the United States.

Trump loved surrounding himself with celebrities and influencers. He wanted to steal their glory and use their successes to his own advantage. What benefit would an up and coming singer be? Not until the singer had achieved success would Trump want him in his camp. By allowing Shawn time to grow into his career, Trump could watch from afar and see if the singer was worth taking on. If not, Trump would walk away and find a different adviser.

By November 2015, Shawn's accolades had grown. He received two MTV music awards, four iHeartRadio awards, a BreakOut award and a People's Choice Award. Further, he had gone down the usual celebrity path and set up a charity campaign, for a cause he knew nothing about.

Trump was impressed. The singer had achieved success and was viewed in the top twenty singers in the world. Now was the time to make his move.

Trump phoned the Russian oligarch Aras Agalarov and asked him to set up a meeting in Russia. Aras complied without question, knowing that Trump would win the Republican primaries and not wanting to refuse the future president.

On 22 November 2015, a secret meeting was arranged in Agalarov's private estate in Kazan, Russia. Shawn Mendes was flown in, believing it to be a meeting with his management. Donald Trump flew in on his private jet.

The details of this meeting are unknown, as the Russians are very skilled at keeping meetings secret. What is known is that after this meeting, Shawn became the loyal adviser to Trump. Further, Shawn Mendes would never tour in Russia, preferring to keep this arrangement discreet.

Chapter Six

The Fallacy of Ted Cruz

'Lyin' Ted Cruz just used a picture of Melania from a G.Q. shoot in his
ad. Be careful, Lyin' Ted, or I will spill the beans on your wife!'
- Donald Trump, 22 March 2016, Twitter.

In 2013, when Hillary Clinton was already preparing her presidency
nomination with Shawn Mendes, political commentators were focusing
on who was going to be the Republican candidate. Most assumed that
Ted Cruz, the young senator from Texas, was expected to run and win.

Aside from being relatively youthful (having been born in 1970),
he was a graduate from Harvard Law School who went on to be the
Texas Attorney General. His ascension to the role of Senator in 2013
was seen as icing on the cake of an illustrious career. Plus, he was of
Hispanic descent and could court the ever-growing Hispanic vote.

Like with most politicians, he was ambitious and wanted the top
job. On 23 March 2015, he announced that he would be running for
the presidential candidacy. He was the first major Republican to
announce. There did not appear to be any other contenders able to
defeat him. Accordingly, sponsors flocked to him. During his
candidacy, he secured over 92 million dollars in funding.

Three months later on 16 June 2015, Donald Trump held a press
conference at Trump Tower. He announced that he would be running
for the candidacy and spoke about immigration, US jobs, debt and
terrorism. His official campaign slogan was 'Make America Great
Again.' Reportedly, on 17 June 2015 Trump phoned Island Records

and informed them that Shawn Mendes should release a song called 'Make America Great Again'. Island Records fortunately rejected this request.

At first, Ted Cruz did not see Donald Trump as a rival. He instead saw him as a bumbling idiot. The man would constantly go into a tirade, and whenever criticised by the media, would slam 'fake news'. From day to day, Trump's stance on issues would change depending on the audience he spoke to. Cruz strongly held the belief that over time the minimal level of support Trump enjoyed would wane.

This was not to be.

Trump was the quintessential anti-establishment candidate. He was campaigning against political correctness and against those on the inside. Never mind that he himself had been on the inside in business circles ever since his birth. This was simply an inconvenient detail.

The media became obsessed with him. Here was a candidate who delivered great sound bites for the evening news. All a journalist had to ask was, 'What will he say next?', and Trump would respond with a biting remark that could create a whole news segment on him. This gave him valuable free press coverage which served to further widen his celebrity-like status. Whereas previously many Republican voters were not overly familiar with Trump or his policies, now they knew his stance.

As time moved on, Trump's support continued to grow so much that he began eclipsing rival candidates. However, Ted Cruz still remained the frontrunner.

Cruz enjoyed the support of senior Republican figures, who were reluctant to place their support behind Trump, who they viewed as unpredictable. In part, this helped Trump widen his support base and add to his anti-establishment credentials.

Whilst Trump was enjoying growing popularity, there was not a single political commentator who believed he stood a chance in the primaries. Even the bookies themselves were writing him off, offering high odds on Trump taking out the election. This would later lead to some very happy pundits.

Donald Trump himself knew that he could not beat Ted Cruz. The man was simply too skilled of an opponent. In order to defeat him, he would need to swap the deck of cards for a more favourable one.

Following on from their Russian meeting, Donald Trump returned to New York with a new chief adviser - Shawn Mendes. As with Hillary, this needed to be kept completely secret. Their communications with one another could not be tracked and there could be no records. Unlike Hillary, Trump did not believe in creating a second email account. Besides, this information on Hillary would later be used by Trump to his own advantage. He would not shoot himself in the foot with her smoking gun.

Trump relied on advice from Shawn Mendes as to how they should communicate. Shawn suggested an easy application - SnapChat. Messages sent between the two of them would disappear after ten seconds, destroying any evidence that they had ever worked together.

Savvy readers by now may be suggesting that there would be evidence of the two working together. Surely Trump was paying Shawn? Would this not be disclosed in Shawn's own tax returns?

The answer is genius. Trump used Island Records to siphon off funds to pay Shawn. Every time Shawn Mendes did a world concert tour, he would be paid for his time as a commission from tickets sold. However, the commission was artificially high. It was being topped up by Trump funds. No tax accountant would have suspected otherwise.

When Shawn arrived on the scene, it was to watch chaos. Trump's campaign was failing. The people beneath Trump were turning on each other, always quick to blame one another. Every single adviser was a yes-man. No matter what Trump's idea, they would nod their heads and quickly action it. Allow Trump to have access to Twitter at night? Sure. Allow Trump to do his own hair styling? Why not.

Shawn could see what the other advisers simply refused to see. Ted Cruz was going to win the primaries. And then he would be defeated by Shawn's old boss, Hillary Clinton. The two were career politicians and Hillary's public persona would give her the edge over Cruz. There would be another four years of Democrat rule, something the now-Republican Trump could simply not abide. They had, after all, destroyed the country and Trump's previous support of the Democrats was completely irrelevant and fake news.

For Shawn, this was also personal. Ted Cruz was a traitor. In August 2013, Cruz had renounced his Canadian citizenship that his mother had bestowed upon him. If there is one thing worse than a Canadian, it is an ex-Canadian. Shawn wanted this man destroyed.

On 25 November 2015, Shawn and Trump met together on the highest level of Trump Tower, within Trump's secret office. The walls were built so that no space satellite could listen in to his conversations. Whether such space technology currently exists is questionable, but Trump Tower is prepared regardless.

Whilst little information is available on what the two discussed, it is clear the main topic was Ted Cruz and how to defeat him. Both men were at a loss. Trump was getting close to quitting as a candidate, worried about the brand damage which would result if he lost to someone like Cruz. Shawn himself was frustrated that he could offer no advice on what to do.

Then Melania Trump walked into the room, carrying a tray of coffee and biscuits. Donald Trump introduced her to Shawn as his machine wife, bringing him into his confidence about the fact that the woman is actually a robot. Shawn was impressed. And then an idea hit him.

What if they were to somehow kill off Ted Cruz and replace him with an exact robot replica? They could then control him, ensuring Trump's victory as candidate.

Trump was not convinced. The plan seemed risky. If it failed and Ted Cruz told the press, it would mean an end to Trump's political career. No voter would support him in the future. To avoid allegations being levelled against him, Trump told Shawn, 'You can proceed with this if you want. But definitely do not include me in it. No way.'

So Shawn Mendes proceeded with a plan to kill Ted Cruz, the Senator from Texas.

The plan was beautiful in its simplicity. Shawn would invite Cruz to Toronto, hinting that he would potentially publicly support his campaign and allow his songs to be used in campaign drives. Cruz would fall for the plan, wanting a celebrity endorsement and fly in to Toronto. Upon his arrival, he would be driven to a secure location to meet with Shawn. The meeting would be kept secret, to protect both of their public images before a deal was decided upon. When Cruz arrived at the location, he would be shot in the head by a hired assassin. His body would then be destroyed using acid, and a replacement robot commissioned in Japan.

And it was a beautiful plan - until everything went wrong.

Initially, Cruz bought the idea and booked a private jet to take him to Toronto. His campaign had momentarily stalled and he believed that Shawn's endorsement would help him with the hard-to-get youth vote. Not to mention, it would present an excellent photography opportunity.

However, when he arrived at the airport his private jet was experiencing technical difficulties and unable to leave. Coincidentally, at the same time David Bowie was in the airport and about to leave for Canada in his jet. Being a generous man, Bowie offered Cruz a lift. Together, the two travelled to Toronto.

The two spoke on the trip about life, politics and music. When Bowie asked Cruz the reason behind going to Canada, Cruz felt comfortable enough to tell him the truth. This interested Bowie greatly. He himself had watched the start of Shawn Mendes' career and was eager to meet the young man. Perhaps he could impose some of his own wisdom on him.

So Bowie tagged along for the car trip to the secure location. When the two men walked in, the assassin shot them both. Both Shawn Mendes and Donald Trump were furious when they found out.

This would be a public relations disaster. David Bowie was popular. Killing him would end a person's presidential aspirations for good. Shawn had to immediately intervene to secure the situation.

David Bowie's body was taken out of Canada and transported to Trump Tower in New York, to await a decision on what to do. It would take Shawn and Donald Trump two months before they finally decided how to reveal to the world that David Bowie had died. Hiring an expert medical professional, his body was altered to make it appear that he died from liver cancer. Then, he was placed in a hotel in New York. He was found by hotel staff on 10 January 2016.

For those who are sceptical that Shawn Mendes accidentally killed David Bowie, ask yourself this. Why was David Bowie's body found in

New York, when he lived in England? Why was his body cremated, instead of him being buried as he wanted? The truth is undeniable. David Bowie stumbled by mistake onto an evil plot and paid for this with his life. Vale, David Bowie.

Whilst they were trying to work out what to do with the body of David Bowie, Ted Cruz was quickly and quietly disposed of. No trace of his human remains were left behind. Within three days, and after Trump's wealth went down by 1.4 million dollars, the robot Ted Cruz arrived in New York City, ready to continue on with his campaign at the behest of Shawn.

As the campaign progressed, political commentators were still convinced that robot Ted Cruz would win.

On 1 February 2016, he won the Iowa caucuses.

On 1 March 2016, he won Texas, Alaska and Oklahoma.

On 5 March 2016, he took out Kansas and Maine. He was now up to six victories.

However, it was not all victories. Trump won Super Tuesday and had a landslide win in Indiana.

The strategy behind keeping Ted Cruz in the race was simple. If Shawn Mendes had dropped the robot Cruz out, then Trump would have won the candidacy far earlier. By keeping him in the race, Trump received more air time and his celebrity status continued to grow. Plus, Cruz's role as an establishment figure also served Trump's interests.

Shawn could clearly see that if Trump managed to defeat robot Cruz, then Trump could easily beat Hillary. It was at this point that Shawn's dominance as a political adviser is shown. No other adviser in the country believed Trump could beat Hillary.

When Cruz lost to Trump in the Indiana primary on 3 May 2016, he announced he would suspend his campaign and no longer continue. The defeat was a landslide loss and it was difficult to see how he could recover from that. Shawn knew that the real Ted Cruz would have pulled out at this point. If he decided to keep the robot Cruz in the race, people would have become suspicious and potentially spotted that the man had been replaced by a machine.

Yet Shawn was playing a dangerous game at this point. He would bring back Ted Cruz into the fold when Trump began to lose popularity, to remind the voters of the establishment candidates. This resulted in Cruz's position over 2016 appearing inconsistent and nonsensical.

For example, despite having suspended his campaign, Cruz made a public statement he would again go for the candidacy if he won the Nebraska primary. If any readers have been to Nebraska, they would know there was no chance Trump would lose here. Cruz's statement was ridiculous, but effective. Trump again received free press and it appeared that he defeated another opponent, even though it was the exact same opponent he had previously defeated.

Robot Cruz would never endorse Trump. To endorse him would be to have the establishment endorse him, which was exactly what Trump and Shawn were avoiding. Shawn carefully leaked to the media stories about Cruz refusing to endorse Trump, which again provided Trump with free press and media coverage.

The biggest move was at the 2016 Republican National Convention, where Trump was officially endorsed as the Republican candidate for presidency. Ted Cruz gave a speech where he congratulated Trump but never endorsed him. Rather, he told voters to, 'vote your conscience, vote for candidates up and down the ticket who you trust to defend our freedom and to be faithful to the Constitution.'

This resulted in booing from the crowd, who saw an establishment figure again telling them what to do. Naturally, they all voted Trump.

When later questioned on this, robot Cruz stated:

> *'I am not in the habit of supporting people who attack my wife and attack my father. That pledge was not a blanket commitment that if you go and slander and attack Heidi, that I'm going to nonetheless come like a servile puppy dog and say, "Thank you very much for maligning my wife and maligning my father."*

Despite this apparent show of bravado, two months later Ted Cruz endorsed Trump, at a time when Trump was facing Hillary. There was no need to keep Cruz from endorsing Trump, now that Trump faced an even bigger establishment figure in Clinton.

Following on from Trump becoming President of the United States, there was some speculation that Ted Cruz would receive the role of Attorney General. This did not eventuate.

Whilst Shawn and Trump did consider making Cruz the Attorney General, they quickly dismissed the idea. True, it would have been helpful to have a Cabinet member they fully controlled like a servile dog, rather than Cabinet members who just acted like servile dogs. But Trump had alienated many Republican lawmakers during his campaign and the damage was irrevocable. Shawn believed that it would prove more useful having a strong ally in the Senate when it came time to pass controversial legislation.

In any event, having a machine replace a human is not always a good idea. At times, their programming can result in their comments being bizarre and embarrassing.

Following on from being replaced by a machine, robot Ted Cruz said the following public quotes (all true, by the way).

On 30 November 2015 he was asked about defunding for Planned Parenthood and responded by saying, 'Last I checked, we don't have a rubber shortage in America. Look, when I was in college, we had a machine in the bathroom, you put 50 cents in and voila.'

When speaking about a shooting, 'We saw the ugly face of radical Islam in Garland, Texas. Thankfully, one police officer helped those terrorists meet their virgins.'

Fortunately for Shawn, Ted Cruz was no stranger to making weird statements before he was killed and replaced with a robot. When he announced his presidency, he made a comment that the world was on fire because of Obama's policies. A three year old girl in the audience thought he was being literal and cried out, asking if they were on fire. Cruz responded directly to the girl by telling her everything is on fire. The girl then broke into hysterics.

Where next, for the robot senator? Will Shawn continue to keep him in the senate? Or are his services better suited to elsewhere? Will the public become suspicious when Ted Cruz's appearance remains the same for twenty years?

It is highly likely that Ted Cruz will again make an appearance in the 2020 election. By all accounts, Donald Trump will contest the next election. In order to win the primaries again, he needs a Republican opponent that people love to hate.

To see whether Shawn puts this plan in action, readers are recommended to follow Ted Cruz's career. When he begins to become vocal in opposition to Trump's policies, that is a sure sign that he is seeking to distance himself in preparation for another tilt at the leadership. He will continue to employ the exact same strategies as before, despite the fact they failed miserably.

By bringing in this establishment figure once more, Republican voters will again turn to Trump for their salvation. And perhaps, by this time, the then-three year old girl will realise that the world is indeed metaphorically on fire.

Chapter Seven

The American Women's
Justice League

'Number one, I have great respect for women.
I was the one that really broke the glass ceiling on behalf of women,
more than anybody else in the construction industry. My relationship I
think is going to end up being very good with women.'
- Donald Trump, 7 June 2016, Fox News Interview.

The year was 2013. Barack Obama had suffered a loss in his administration with the departure of Hillary Clinton. His popularity was slipping and the public began questioning whether he could get things done. Hillary, who had started the year so well by unofficially launching her candidacy campaign, ended the year in chaos, having sacked her best adviser. And Donald Trump, the threat no one saw coming, had commenced his plan to take on Shawn Mendes as an adviser.

A grim year, to be sure. It seemed there was no hope for the Democrats, they just did not know it yet.

Yet out of the fire, new life can be born. And it was here at the end of 2013, that hope was kindled.

The First Lady of the United States, Michelle LaVaughn Robinson Obama, could see that the Republicans were beginning to gain traction. She could see her husband's legacy was threatened. And she could see that there was a hidden threat no one was yet aware of.

Michelle Obama, another graduate of Harvard Law School, sensed something was off. It is highly unlikely that at this stage she was aware of Donald Trump's plan. All she knew was she needed to take action before it was too late.

Did Michelle confide in her husband about her concerns? No. Barack was incredibly busy at this time and did not have any capacity to fight an unknown threat. As First Lady, Michelle viewed it as her sworn duty to fix the situation. Otherwise, her husband's lasting impact would be lost throughout the ages.

Pledging to uncover what was going on, Michelle immediately set out investigating. She knew she could not do this alone. Whether it was a Republican-wide plot or a rogue Republican, something was up.

On 18 December 2013, Michelle Obama hosted a dinner at the White House. She invited only two guests. Ellen DeGeneres and Carrie Fisher, two of America's most influential women.

Michelle sat at the head of the table, laughing at a joke Ellen told. Carrie chuckled quietly, sipping on a glass of red wine.

'I hope you are hungry,' Michelle said, as the waiters brought out the plates of pan-fried salmon and salad. 'This salmon is fresh this morning.'

'Smells delicious,' Carrie said.

'So tell me, Michelle,' Ellen said. 'Have you ever woken up during the night and had the kitchen make you something?'

'Only the once,' Michelle said, smiling indulgently. 'A year ago. I just had a massive craving for eggs hollandaise. By the time they made it, I was no longer hungry, but I felt so guilty that I had to eat it.'

'First world problems, right there,' Ellen said. 'Or elite first world problems?'

'I'm sure you didn't invite us here to talk about your kitchen staff,' Carrie said, stabbing her knife into the salmon. 'Not that I'm ungrateful. But I can't say I normally get an invite here.'

'You are correct. I invited you both here, as the three of us collectively would hold more influence than anyone else in America.'

'A pop culture icon,' Ellen said, gesturing towards Carrie.

'A comic genius,' Michelle said, nodding at Ellen.

'And a political great and fashion icon,' Carrie said towards Michelle.

'You're too kind,' she replied. 'But essentially, yes. Together, the three of us would have the power to exercise great change.'

'I don't really get involved in politics,' Carrie said. 'If you've invited us here to back your husband, I'm afraid that won't be happening.'

Ellen frowned, 'Are you considering running in 2016, Michelle?'

Michelle laughed, 'No. That is far too soon. Barack needs me here for support. If I were to run, I would need him for support. We cannot have two presidents in the family at the same time. We could not handle that.'

'But someday in the future perhaps?'

'Perhaps. But that is still not why I have brought you here. As we speak, the Republicans are preparing something big. We need to take action.'

'Like I said, I don't get involved in politics,' Carrie said.

'This transcends politics. It even transcends the Republican and Democrat parties.'

'How so?' Ellen asked.

'There is some force at work. Something dark is being plotted.'

'Sounds like a bunch of bullshit to me,' Carrie said, finishing her glass and calling on the waiter for some more.

'I know it sounds stupid. But a lot of things have happened this year that do not make sense.'

'Such as?' Ellen asked.

'Hillary resigned. She told me that she was not planning on running for president again. I believed her. She was not lying. This sudden departure of hers seems out of character. Besides, it is far too early for her to leave, even if her original plan was to run in 2016. That's three years away.'

'One decision does not equal a dark force,' Carrie remarked.

'True, but Hillary launched on Facebook this year. She has become a powerful social media influencer. Most don't understand how she has been able to do it. She never previously had any social media skills. Bernie came to my office asking if I knew whether she had appointed any special adviser and if he could get a similar one. I told him I had no idea. Which is true.'

'So she decided to quit and found some super duper adviser. Big deal,' Carrie said.

'That's not all. Donald Trump has once again cut off funding to the Democrats.'

'He does that all the time,' Ellen said, waving her hand dismissively. 'One year he is a Republican, then a Democrat, then an eggplant. Why would it mean anything now?'

'Because this year he has begun acting oddly. He took the Miss Universe Pageant to Moscow. Why Moscow? The Russians do not mean anything to him.'

'I don't like Russians,' Carrie said.

'And the strangest thing of all... Malia is suddenly obsessed with this Vine singer. I can't quite remember his name. Shawn Men I think.'

'Your daughter Malia?'

'Yes. She's always going on about him being the next big thing. She thinks that Island Records are looking at signing him up. I looked them up. They're a British company, but the State Department thinks that they may be getting Russian funding. None of it makes sense.'

'So what do you want us to do?'

'Keep your ears to the ground. If you hear anything, no matter how irrelevant you think it is, let me know. We need to remain vigilant.'

'We'll be like the Justice League,' Carrie snorted.

'The American Women's Justice League,' Ellen corrected.

The two women did not take Michelle Obama seriously on that night, when the AWJL was formed. However, neither dared to refuse the First Lady and decided to humour her request.

Over 2014, the AWJL remained quiet. Neither woman reported anything to Michelle. Ellen was busy with her show and Carrie was busy filming the next *Star Wars* movie.

In 2015, when Donald Trump announced he was running for the candidacy, Michelle's worst fears were confirmed. She, unlike so many others, suspected that Trump would beat Ted Cruz. And she could envision that if elected, he would tear down everything her husband had built.

Carrie Fisher was still busy in 2015 and did not share Michelle's fear for the future. She could not believe that Donald Trump would win the presidency and ignored any messages she received from Michelle or Ellen.

Ellen similarly doubted that the public would place their trust in Trump, but she was willing to help Michelle in any way she could. She had Michelle visit her show, boosting Michelle's profile and introducing her humour to a whole new audience. The segment was a hit and Michelle's popularity grew.

When Michelle could, she publicly supported Hillary, hoping that by throwing her own popularity behind the Clintons she would hurt Trump in the polls. Her famous line, 'When they go low, we go high,' was a hit, but failed to have a significant impact. By involving herself in the Clinton campaign, Michelle distracted herself, rendering her unable to have any meaningful act in thwarting Trump and Shawn's campaign.

If only she had listened to Malia Obama in 2013, when she had become a fan of Shawn Mendes, Michelle may have been able to fit the puzzle together and realise what was going on. It was not to be.

Whilst Michelle and Ellen continued to do what they could, Carrie carried on with filming for *Star Wars*. Carrie Fisher is known as a dedicated actress who gets completely involved with her character, doing anything possible to immerse herself in the role.

For those readers unfamiliar with the *Star Wars* films, they are based in a universe heavily populated by various creatures and droids. The human characters in the film rely heavily on their droid allies for everyday tasks, from helping to pilot spaceships to acting as waiters.

Carrie wanted to learn more about droids and machines, so she took a short holiday to Japan in late 2016. It was here that she met a certain Japanese inventor, who specialised in creating machines which looked exactly like humans. Unfortunately, the inventor had recently been diagnosed with cancer and only had a few short months left to live.

For any person that has met Carrie, she has a certain personality that results in people trusting her immediately. The inventor felt that when he met her he saw in her his chance for redemption. He decided to confess that in the past he had created two robots for Donald Trump. One to act as Melania Trump. The other to replace the murdered Ted Cruz.

In one of life's rare moments where everything seems to just fall into place, Carrie had stumbled upon the truth that Michelle was seeking for in 2013. Her eyes widening, Carrie now knew that Michelle was right.

As soon as she returned to her hotel, Carrie tried to make a phone call to Michelle, but she did not answer. Her only other option was to call Ellen, who answered within three rings.

Unfortunately, the date was 27 September 2016. For any Shawn Mendes followers out there, they will realise this is the date he appeared on Ellen's show. She answered the call as she was talking to Shawn in the make-up room.

Ellen did not know that she had to be suspicious of Shawn Mendes. If she had, she would not have repeated word for word what Carrie told her.

A source told your correspondent in an exclusive interview that the conversation lasted thirty seconds. Further:

> 'Yeah, it was a quick conversation. Ellen told Carrie that she was about to start filming. Carrie said something quickly, then Ellen hung up the phone. Afterwards, she turned to Shawn and was like, "That was Carrie Fisher. She wants to talk to me when she gets back in the US. Apparently she's discovered some evil robot making scientist in Japan. I swear she is losing it." Shawn laughed awkwardly and then they changed the story to Dory or something.'

Carrie Fisher would never make it back to another phone. Before she could even board the plane, she was captured by Trump-paid agents. On 27 December 2016, it was announced to the world that Carrie Fisher died from cardiac arrest.

That was a lie.

Carrie Fisher, the only member of the AWJL who uncovered the truth, is currently being kept prisoner in Trump Tower. Accounts differ on the state of her health, as Shawn makes sure that Trump changes his staff regularly to avoid any infiltration within the building. It is almost impossible to uncover a roster and determine which staff member will be near Carrie Fisher at what time.

However, in a further exclusive, it can be revealed that Carrie Fisher is being kept in a frozen state in the highest level of Trump

Tower. What Trump's plan is for her is unclear. Why did he not have her killed like he did with Ted Cruz? Was it because he had escaped bad publicity surrounding David Bowie's murder, and did not want to test his luck twice? Or is there, perhaps, a chance for Carrie Fisher to be unfrozen in time for the 2020 election, and announced as his running mate?

Time will tell.

Chapter Eight

Build It And They Will [Not] Come

'You have a bunch of bad hombres down there. You aren't doing enough to stop them. I think your military is scared. Our military isn't, so I might just send them down to take care of it.'
- Donald Trump, 2 February 2017,
Conversation with the President of Mexico.

When Donald Trump launched his campaign for candidacy in June 2015, one of the core themes of his speech was Mexico.

'When Mexico sends its people, they're not sending their best. They're sending people that have lots of problems… They're bringing drugs. They're bringing crime. They're rapists.'

Trump took the view that the average voter was against Mexican rapists. And how could anyone argue against his position of anti-rape? It seemed, to Trump at least, to be the perfect election-winning strategy.

In order to prevent these Mexican rapists from entering the country, he promised to build a huge wall across the 2,000 mile long border.

'I will build a great, great wall on our southern border, and I will have Mexico pay for that wall. Mark my words,' he promised.

So not only was Trump going to save the USA from Mexican rapists, he was also going to do it at zero cost to the taxpayer. Mexico would be honoured to pay for the full cost of one of Trump's policies.

The question posed by journalists at the time was why would Mexico ever agree to pay for such a costly wall that was not in their interests? What possible leverage did Trump have over the entire nation of Mexico that would propel them to send billions of dollars to the US?

At the time, Mexico lashed back. They were not going to pay for the wall, and 'the remarks by Donald Trump seem prejudicial and absurd,' the Mexican Interior Minister said.

However, it was Trump's view that Mexico could pay for the wall, as they were 'ripping off the US more than almost any other nation' and were continuing 'to make billions of dollars in remittances sent from illegal immigrants in the United States.' So not only were the Mexicans coming to the US to rape, but they were also removing billions of dollars from the economy.

Suddenly, a wall seemed like a very good idea.

Many Republican voters actually liked the proposal. The US has always had problems with immigrants, from the Mexicans to the terrible Canadians. And, as Trump pointed out, the Great Wall of China is over 13,000 miles long. If the Chinese could build a wall, surely the Americans could build one only 2,000 miles.

It was estimated that the cost of building the wall would be between 15 billion dollars to 25 billion dollars, with an annual upkeep of 700 million dollars. If Mexico refused to pay for the wall, it would be a costly exercise for a nation already crippled by debt.

Even if Mexico refused to pay, Trump would simply seize remittances from illegal Mexican immigrants and increase fees on entry visas from Mexicans travelling to the US. Simple.

Throughout the campaign, Mexico continued to publicly state they would not pay for the wall. Trump continued to say that they would.

In 2016 he stated, 'We will build a great wall along the Southern border and Mexico will pay for the wall. One hundred percent. They don't know it yet but they're going to pay for it.'

The plan was soundly criticised by Democrats and anti-Trump Republicans, who did not believe the plan would work. After all, in places where fencing currently exists along the border, Mexican drug smugglers have a system of tunnels in place to circumvent the wall. Why would they simply not expand these tunnels if a wall was built?

At the time of writing, President Trump has maintained his commitment to build the wall. Presently, prototypes of the material are being tested for strength and, should they pass, the wall will be built. Mexico is still refusing to fund any aspect of the wall.

All political experts are in agreement that Trump's promise to build the wall helped him in the polls and resonated with his core supporter base. Without this policy, Trump may not have been elected President.

So what did drive Trump to target the Mexican rapists? Was it his hatred of all things Mexican? Was it his cunning political instinct? Or was it something else entirely?

For those readers suggesting that it was Shawn Mendes who came up with the idea, they would be very wrong indeed. At the time Trump made this election commitment, Shawn was not advising Trump. It would not be until five months later that Shawn was hired. Something else was at play here.

Trump used Mexican rapists as a cover for the real purpose of building the wall. There was a person he wanted to keep out of the US for good, and he believed that a wall was the only solution. The political gain and poll boost was only a secondary factor in his decision. No one would question his decision. He was, after all, a Republican. And Republicans do not generally like Mexicans.

So who was this one person Trump was prepared to build an entire wall to keep out? Who was this one person Trump feared above all others? Who would keep Trump awake at night, fearing what he would do next?

James Corden.

Publicly, James Corden is a television host of the popular '*The Late Late Show with James Corden*'. Born on 22 August 1978 in London, he was always attracted to the arts. From a young age he performed in theatre shows before progressing to television work in the late 1990s. His career continued to flourish in the 21st Century, where he starred in the British show '*Fat Friends*'. Inventing Carpool Karaoke, he takes famous singers through the streets whilst they sing along to the radio. Despite sounding ridiculous, it has been a great hit.

Launched in 2015, the celebrities who have appeared on the segment are: Mariah Carey, Jennifer Hudson, Justin Bieber, Iggy Azalea, Rod Stewart, Stevie Wonder, Jason Derulo, Carrie Underwood, One Direction, Adele, Chris Martin, Elton John, Sia, Jennifer Lopez, Gwen Stefani, Demi Lovato, Nick Jonas, Red Hot Chilli Peppers, Selena Gomez, Michelle Obama, Britney Spears, Lady GaGa, Madonna, Bruno Mars, George Martin, Stephen Curry, Harry Styles, Katy Perry, Ed Sheeran, Usher, and Miley Cyrus.

Savvy readers will notice two things about the above list. One, it excludes loyal ally Shawn Mendes. And secondly, it includes founder of the American Women's Justice League, Michelle Obama.

This leads to the key question. Why would James Corden exclude Shawn Mendes from his segment? Why would he invite a known enemy of Trump, namely Michelle Obama, to appear on a singing segment when she is not in fact a singer?

Yes, the answer is obvious. James Corden, since 2010, has secretly been the President of Mexico. His real name is actually James Cordén. However, this in itself does not reveal why Trump would want to keep the Mexican President out of the USA. What did secret-President Cordén do to upset Trump so greatly that he would spend billions of dollars on keeping him out?

The two have been long-time rivals in the real estate industry. Corden would regularly assume other identities to thwart Trump's plans. Whilst no one else realised Corden was behind it, Trump knew and resented him for it.

In 1978, the year Corden was born, Trump purchased a half-share in the Commodore Hotel in New York. He would remodel the hotel and then rename it the Grand Hyatt Hotel. In this same year, he commenced developing Trump Tower, which would be completed in 1983, the year Corden turned five.

In 1988, Trump purchased the Plaza Hotel. He refitted the hotel and sold it for a record profit in 1995.

In 1996, he bought the Bank of Manhattan Trust Building and then renamed it the Trump Building at 40 Wall Street.

In 1997, he began constructing Trump Place. This caught the attention of Corden, who was now nineteen years old and was passionate about real estate and the arts. Corden, who himself had always wanted to commence a development and name it Trump Place for reasons best known to himself, became insanely jealous.

The development was riddled with delays. Most notably, defective concrete was used and it had to be replaced. What is not publicly known is that Corden was the mastermind behind the defective concrete. He secretly paid off the subcontractors to install defective products, hoping that Trump would abandon the project and move on.

This was not to be. Trump realised that someone was working against him and this made him even more determined to finish the project. Despite Corden's numerous attempts at sabotage, the development was sold in 2005 for 1.8 billion dollars. A record sum.

Corden may have lost to Trump in this scenario, but he was not to be deterred.

Empire State Building, one of New York's most impressive buildings, was half-owned by Trump from 1994 to 2002. It was Trump's desire to rename it the '*Trump Empire State Building Tower Apartments*'. However, Corden through a variety of trust funds and offshore entities owned the other half-share of the building. He resisted every single one of Trump's attempts at renaming the building. By 2002, Trump abandoned the attempt and sold off his share. He would never forgive Corden for this slight.

All of this was water under the bridge for the two real estate moguls. Throughout his life, Trump had his eyes set on the presidency, just as Corden has his eyes set on the Mexican presidency.

Trump believed that he would need to set up a team of loyal staffers if he was ever to take the presidency. However, he wanted these staffers to be educated and indoctrinated in his beliefs. To do so, he set up Trump University on 23 May 2005. This for-profit education company ran a real estate course until 2010, when it would become defunct after a variety of lawsuits were filed against it.

Trump University was never an accredited university or college and did not offer any credit to its students. The New York Attorney General sued the University for illegal business practices on the basis that students were misled by advertising Trump University as an actual university.

One student, who will remain nameless, provided this evidence to your correspondent:

> *'I went to Trump University from 2006 to 2008. I got a Trump Degree in Trumpnomics, which sounded really cool at the time. Where am I working at the moment? McDonald's. Yeah, no one wanted to hire me despite having gone there. I thought I was going there to learn how to be a billionaire and stuff, but most of the time we just watched re-runs of Celebrity Apprentice and rated contestants for Miss Universe. We got to play a lot of fun games though. Every Friday night there was a themed night at Trump Pub, which was 'Pin the Penis on the Mexican Rapist'. And then there was trivial pursuit every Wednesday. That one was pretty easy to win. All of the answers were just Donald Trump.'*

Naturally, after graduating and finding out that their qualification was all but useless, many students complained to authorities. These complaints fell on deaf ears. Many within the New York government had received financial support from Trump during their elections. They did not want to upset the man they relied upon for support.

Enter James Cordén, the secret-Mexican President. Corden decided to make it his mission in life to destroy Trump University. Using his own real estate interests, he compelled a New York prosecutor to file a claim against Trump. Accordingly, Corden used his influence to ensure that Judge Gonzalo P. Curiel was appointed to oversee the case.

For those who may recall, Trump criticised the Judge during the election campaign, alleging bias on the basis of his Mexican heritage. Trump was of the view that the Judge could not objectively hear the case, given he was part-Mexican and Trump was promising to build a wall to keep the Mexicans (or one Mexican in particular) out.

Because of all of the lawsuits, Trump University ceased to exist in 2010. After becoming President, Trump settled the remaining cases for a total of 25 million dollars. James Corden had succeeded.

Trump University was the feather in Trump's cap and he could never forgive Corden for destroying it. This was a huge blow to his ego and hurt his plan of creating a legion of loyal staffers all of whom had been trained within his own educational facility. Further, it also put an end to a policy idea of renaming every university in the USA to Trump

University. Harvard Law School was intended to become Trumpard Law School.

Trump feared what Corden would do next. Would he target Trump Tower? Would he try to steal Melania away from him, the loyal robot in his service?

This is why he promised to build a wall. It was Trump's reasoning that if he built a massive wall along the border, Corden would no longer be able to get into the US to host his television show and his influence in the states would be reduced remarkably. Thus, an enemy would be removed.

But Corden was not going to go down without a fight. He invited Michelle Obama, leader of the AWJL, to attend his carpool karaoke. There was no logic behind having Michelle on the show. She was not a singer. She was the First Lady. No First Lady in history had ever attended a singing show before, which struck some commentators as a bizarre turn of events. Corden was sending Trump a clear message of where his support would be placed during the election.

Trump retaliated accordingly. He called up Island Records and informed them that Shawn Mendes would not be allowed to attend Carpool Karaoke. He told them to send Nick Jonas instead, hoping to sabotage the show.

Did Corden know that Shawn was an adviser to Trump? Possibly. As the secret-Mexican President, Corden had access to an entire intelligence agency that was tracking Trump's every movement. Therefore it is conceivable Corden uncovered the truth. This could be why he had Justin Bieber, Shawn's natural enemy, appear on the show twice.

For readers who watch Corden's show, they would be up in arms at this point. If the above is true, why did Shawn Mendes appear on Corden's show? Sure, he may never have appeared on Carpool Karaoke, but he has appeared on the show itself. Twice, in fact.

The most notable appearance was on 23 November 2015, one day after Shawn was engaged by Trump as his adviser. I invite those sceptical readers to watch the episode from 23 November 2015, where Shawn Mendes and Camila Cabello attended. Aside from the negative body language being cast off by Shawn during the show, readers will observe the following exchange:

James Corden: Shawn, you have had the most incredible year [sarcastic tone of voice used].

...

Camila Cabello: I just got back from rehearsals, as we are going to go to Mexico tomorrow, which is really exciting.

Shawn looks down in disgust.

James Corden: Great!

Crowd cheers in support.

...

James Corden: You're saying no, can I be honest, I don't believe you.

Shawn Mendes: Well I don't care.

The tension between Corden and Shawn is obvious to anyone watching. It is apparent that the two are facing off in a Trump exchange, which is why Corden invited a Mexican singer to attend.

Despite these encounters, there was no major bad blood between Shawn and Corden. This was reserved for Corden and Trump, who would continue to fight it out during the election using third parties as their weapons.

Now that Trump is President of the United States, it raises some concerns for secret-Mexican President Cordén. Will this permanently affect relations between the two countries? Will this have a negative impact on the economy? Will President Trump and President Cordén be able to reconcile their differences and work together for the benefit of their two nations?

No. This feud is for eternity and no diplomat is skilled enough to reconcile the two men. Unfortunately, this means that the wall will be built on the border. Billions of dollars will be spent on concrete, bricks and fencing under the pretence of keeping Mexican rapists out of the

US, with the real purpose to keep secret-Mexican President Cordén out of the US.

When asked to comment on this, Corden refused all requests for an interview.

Those within the Trump camp believe that Corden is now the one afraid. They say that once the wall is complete, he will no longer be able to host his television show and he will lose access to all of his shady real estate deals in New York. His empire will be in tatters and he will begin to lose his support base within Mexico, meaning that a coup will occur. Corden will be stuck in Mexico with the rapists the USA deported, left with nothing but a bitter taste in his mouth.

No celebrity is prepared to do Carpool Karaoke in the streets of Mexico City, fearing for their life. Whilst David Bowie may have been prepared to venture there, his murder at the hands of the assassin prevents this from occurring. The only guest willing to do it would be that one member of One Direction no one speaks about anymore. The total YouTube views on this segment? Three.

And what does Corden's camp believe? Are they fearful that the wall will stop him from entering the US and his career will be over, all thanks to Donald Trump? Well, he does own a private jet so all he has to do is fly over the wall.

Chapter Nine

Trump's Real Wife

'If I were running "The View", I'd fire Rosie O'Donnell.
I mean, I'd look at her right in that fat, ugly face of hers,
I'd say "Rosie, you're fired.'
- Donald Trump, 23 August 2006,
Entertainment Tonight Interview.

As readers will recall, Trump has had three marriages during his lifetime. In 1977 he married Ivana, in 1993 he married Maria, and in 2005 he married Melania. The third marriage to Melania is not legitimate as, at this stage, humans and machines are unable to be legally married.

Melania's purpose is to act as a beautiful and well dressed partner to Trump. Additionally, she is a skilled killing machine and acts as his bodyguard when situations go awry.

But Trump loves women. He has made no secret of this in the past. There is a 2005 recording where Trump brags about forcibly kissing women and groping them. He said, 'I just start kissing them. I don't even wait. And when you're a star, they let you do it, you can do anything… grab them by the pussy.' He is also a firm believer that he has the status to seduce women.

During the election campaign, fifteen women came out publicly with allegations of sexual misconduct against him. Trump vehemently denied all such claims. Unfortunately, in American politics there is no way of telling whether the smears are true or not. It is often the case that people are paid off to make allegations, in an attempt to discredit an opponent.

Whether those allegations are true or not does not detract from the fact that Trump has always had a relationship with beautiful women. Be it through his various marriages or his ownership of the *Miss Universe Pageant*. The fact is that he always needs to surround himself with attractive, human women.

Melania is not human. She cannot satisfy Trump in this area. Whilst she acts as a great tool to his political ambitions and saves funds on Secret Service personnel, she cannot help him in the bedroom.

On the night of their wedding in 2005, Trump did not share a hotel room with Melania. She was standing guard outside his door, as she normally does. On this night, Trump was with a woman he had been with for three months - Rosie O'Donnell.

Readers will doubt this claim. Rosie O'Donnell and Donald Trump are known arch-rivals. They have hated each other since 2006. The feud has been public and longstanding. Not to mention, Rosie O'Donnell is a lesbian and Donald Trump is a man. This does not match.

But does it?

As a background to the feud, it is alleged to have commenced on 19 December 2006. Trump made a decision to not fire Miss USA Tara Conner after it was revealed she had engaged in drug use, underage drinking and sexual activities. Trump said that he believed in second chances and he was not going to take her crown away. Instead, he sent her to rehab.

On 20 December 2006, Rosie O'Donnell, who was co-host of 'The View' criticised this decision and stated that she did not like Trump. She also made mention that Trump had gone bankrupt (sidenote: Donald Trump has never been personally bankrupt. He did once come close, but he has never filed for personal bankruptcy.)

Rosie O'Donnell went one step further. She said:

> *'Trump is not a self-made man, but a snake-oil salesman on Little House on the Prairie. He left the first wife - had an affair. He had kids both times, but he has the moral compass for 20 year olds in America. Donald, sit and spin, my friend.'*

Because of this, it is often viewed that Rosie O'Donnell started the feud between the two. Donald Trump, as is his wont, responded immediately by calling O'Donnell a 'real loser' and labelled her a 'woman out of control'.

Trump then made a claim that he would sue O'Donnell for the false statements made against him. As he said, 'I look forward to taking lots of money from my nice fat little Rosie'. This was controversial, as most consider it poor form to call a woman fat, even if she is.

So why would the two have had this public argument if they had been in a relationship for over a year? This is because they had a private argument and, given that they both have larger-than-life personalities, they were unable to keep their private lives private. The spat extended into the public realm.

A source close to the pair revealed that they were both like wildfire, saying:

> 'Donald and Rosie are madly in love with each other, to the point of insanity. They have one of the weirdest relationships I have ever seen. They fight like crazy, then go and make angry love. I think they enjoy the arguments with each other. They get off on it. One day they will be super happy, the next day they will be screaming at each other. Every argument always goes way too far. Then they can't help themselves but make it public. They keep their relationship private, but not their fights. It's funny in a way.'

This is most shown in May 2007, when O'Donnell left her job as co-host of 'The View' because she had a heated spat with her fellow co-host over the Iraq war. O'Donnell was strongly against the war.

Trump immediately leapt to his lover's defence, publicly stating:

> 'On this one I think Rosie should win, but Rosie is not much herself. I think anybody that's against the war in Iraq is the winner of the fight, because to justify the war in Iraq - only an imbecile could do that.'

This was a sudden change of heart to the public. Whereas previously Trump had lashed out at O'Donnell, now he was taking her side. However, most readers would acknowledge that it is normal for a partner to want to publicly defend the other when they are under attack. It would have been stranger if Trump had remained silent and allowed O'Donnell to suffer alone.

Following this, the two continued to fight and reconcile on numerous occasions. In one such fight, O'Donnell told Trump that she was leaving him for good.

Because of their jilted relationship, O'Donnell wanted to hurt Trump as much as possible. So she left him for a woman and in December 2011 announced her engagement to Michelle Rounds.

Trump immediately went on Twitter and said, 'I feel sorry for Rosie's new partner in love whose parents are devastated at the thought of their daughter being with Rosie - a true loser.'

O'Donnell then lashed back and tweeted, 'Wow u r an ass in every way.'

Whilst most people simply viewed this as an extension of their public feud, it was clear that the two were going through a difficult separation.

Hurting badly from her betrayal, Trump then tweeted criticism of O'Donnell's new show and labelled it a 'complete and total disaster.' He also said, 'It's really amazing. When I don't like somebody their shows do really badly.'

The break-up between the two would continue into the early months of 2012, when the presidential election was occurring and Barack Obama was seeking a second term. The singer Cher, in May 2012, decided to slam the Republican candidate Mitt Romney.

Trump viewed this as another opportunity to criticise his lover. He tweeted, 'Cher attacked Mitt Romney. She is an average talent who is out of touch with reality. Like Rosie O'Donnell, a total loser!'

However, the next month the two reconciled and were once again together, having regular sexual intercourse in Trump Tower.

In August 2012, Rosie O'Donnell suffered from a heart attack during an especially fiery sexual encounter between her and Trump.

Trump, feeling incredibly guilty, tweeted, 'Rosie, get better fast. I'm starting to miss you!'

As previously stated, Trump always requires the company of a woman and could not last for long if O'Donnell was in hospital for an extended period. O'Donnell responded on Twitter with, 'Well thank u

Donald - I must admit ur post was a bit of a shock… R u trying to kill me ? xx.'

This was a minor slip-up from O'Donnell. Their relationship was supposed to remain quiet, but here she was publicly sending Trump the kiss symbol at the end of a message. Fortunately, no member of the public picked up on it.

For a short period, they were once again a happy couple. Then in April 2014 they had a fight and their spat went public.

In the previous month, O'Donnell gave a speech where she revealed her weight loss following surgery. In April, Trump tweeted, 'Rosie O'Donnell just said she felt "shame" at being fat - not politically correct! She killed Star Jones for weight loss surgery, just had it!'

O'Donnell responded with, 'Donald - go away.'

This spat was short-lasting. The two made up and when O'Donnell returned to 'The View' in July 2014, Trump tweeted his support for the move, saying that it was a clever decision by ABC. He also added that her inclusion in the show would have a short term positive effect. The two lovers were once again happy.

In a sign of their love-hate relationship, Trump tweeted, 'Rosie is crude, rude, obnoxious and dumb - other than that I like her very much!' It takes a special kind of relationship for a person to love the flaws about their partner.

Then in September 2014, O'Donnell revealed that the criticism from Trump affected her deeply. O'Donnell said, 'Probably the Trump stuff was the most bullying I ever experienced in my life, including as a child. It was national, and it was sanctioned societally. Whether I deserved it is up to your own interpretation.'

Clearly, Trump's opinion mattered to O'Donnell. Every public figure receives criticism from all angles. They are immune to most. It is only criticism from people close to them that really hurts.

Trump tweeted back, 'Rosie - no offence, and good luck on the new show, but remember, you started it!'

Who started the argument is an age old question between couples. Both partners want to be right and cannot stand it when the other is.

When Trump announced his candidacy for presidency in June 2015, O'Donnell was a firm supporter in the background. She provided advice and support to him until Shawn Mendes was engaged in November. Without her, it is unlikely that Trump would have survived the first few months.

In the first Republican presidential primary debate in August 2015, Trump was asked whether his use of language like 'dogs', 'slobs' and 'fat pigs' to describe women was acceptable. Trump responded by saying, 'Only Rosie O'Donnell.' Within minutes, O'Donnell tweeted, 'Try explaining that 2 ur kids.'

What did she mean by this? To whose kids? None other than the son of Donald Trump and Rosie O'Donnell - Baron Trump. Whilst most do not know that O'Donnell is Baron's mother, this is the only logical explanation for his birth. Melania, as a machine, cannot have children. In fact, his whole name is a play on words. Melania is barren given she does not have any internal reproductive organs. Trump was amused when naming his son, as the public would never realise that Baron's name is meant as an ironic joke on the claim that Melania gave birth to him.

In September 2016, Trump faced off against Hillary in a debate. Hillary criticised Trump for the way he speaks to women, not realising that Trump and O'Donnell were lovers.

Trump responded by saying, 'Hillary is hitting me with tremendous commercials. Some of it I said in entertainment, some of it said to somebody who has been very vicious to me, Rosie O'Donnell. I said very tough things to her and I think everybody would agree she deserves it and nobody feels sorry for her.'

O'Donnell then tweeted that Trump would never become president and asked people to 'shame the Donald'. Again, the two were having a public fight.

Trump, who normally plays his cards very close to his chest, has been remarkably open in his public spats with O'Donnell. The press has failed to reveal this relationship, which goes to show that investigative journalism is dead.

Most have simply put down the spat to a long time hatred that has refused to blow over. However, this explanation is ridiculous. Why would a billionaire and a comedian hate each other so much if they were not lovers? Why would this fight continue over the space of four years and never end? Why would Trump single out a comedian during his presidential debates, if she was not always on his mind?

The two have spent an inordinately amount of time on each other online, constantly sending out Tweets to get stuck into each other. Whilst this could be explained if it happened just the once, it regularly occurs. Both seem to enjoy the fight.

When Donald Trump won the election and was announced as the next President, O'Donnell tweeted 'God help us all.' She did this because she knew that Trump's powers would increase, meaning that their future disagreements would become even more popular.

Of more pressing concern to O'Donnell was how they would now meet. She could not stay at the White House. This would reveal the nature of their relationship and potentially expose Melania as a robot. Besides, O'Donnell had little to do with Baron Trump and found it awkward to be near her son.

When Trump visits New York, the two meet in Trump Tower and enjoy each other's company. However, O'Donnell does not visit Washington D.C., which has put a considerable strain on their relationship.

Source close to O'Donnell believe that the relationship may not survive the presidency. They have said:

> 'Rosie still loves Donald, but she just does not see how this is going to work. They cannot go public with it. Imagine the scandal if the President gets a divorce whilst in office! And they can't really keep it private anymore. It is all too hard. Everything Donald does is closely watched. I don't know what is going to happen, but Rosie is very upset by all of this.'

And what about O'Donnell's female partners? Are they aware that she is in a secret relationship with the President of the United States?

No. O'Donnell keeps this aspect of her life to herself. Not even her family is aware that she and Trump are close. Just like Trump, she knows how to keep a secret and refuses to disclose it to anyone aside from her closest friends, who assist with setting up the meeting times for her and Trump.

Rumour has it that Trump considered making O'Donnell the Secretary of Defence, to provide her with an excuse to visit Washington and the White House. He believed that her credentials as a media personality would make her perfect to lead the country's defence, as no one would be able to predict her next move. 'Unpredictability is the best offence,' Trump is said to have remarked.

However, Shawn Mendes soundly rejected this idea, telling Trump that this would be political suicide and the military would never accept O'Donnell as their Secretary of Defence. Reluctantly, Trump abandoned this idea.

So what next for the happy couple? Will they split up, bowing to the pressures of the highest office of the land? Or will they continue to have their love affair, as restricted as it is? Will Baron Trump ever realise that his mother is Rosie O'Donnell?

Some people are of the view that Trump will not be able to stand being away from O'Donnell for so long. There is a school of thought that he will, at some point, decide to resign from the presidency under the pretence of wanting to spend more time with his family. By family, he means Rosie O'Donnell.

This would likely occur in an impeachment-type scenario. No public statements relating to O'Donnell will be released, but the true purpose behind it would be clear.

Donald gasps like a wounded gazelle after finishing, holding the blanket up to his chin and staring up at the ceiling.

'I am the best lover ever. The best ever. No one is better than me at making love. No one.'

'Oh, Donald, you truly are a terrible person,' Rosie pants from next to him. 'It's been so long.'

'I can't be in New York all the time, love. People want me everywhere. People love me. It's hard being me. Everyone wants me.'

'But I have you,' she said.

'Yes, you do. You're a pig. An obnoxious pig. But you are my obnoxious pig. All mine.'

'You shouldn't call me that. It's rude.'

'Yes, you're rude too. Very rude. And I am the greatest. By far the greatest.'

'When will we get to see each other again?'

'I don't know. I'll try not to make it too long this time. But no promises. I'm a very important person. The most important man. Everybody wants me.'

Rosie O'Donnell offers Trump an escape from his life. She is the only person to not judge him, but to accept him as another human being. While the pair may have their fair share of arguments, the fact is they always come back to each other afterwards. No matter what is said between them, they forgive each other.

These love-hate relationships are quite common in celebrity circles. It is a strange phenomenon that exists amongst those who love fame and enjoy being spoken about. Scientists believe that it commonly occurs with narcissists who are prone to be aggressive towards the object of their love. Narcissists enjoy the thrill of the fight and being able to prepare their next line. In some circumstances, only hate and love exist as the emotions between them. It is also believed that low self-esteem can cause these relationships.

There are some other famous celebrity couples who have had love-hate relationships that the press are obsessed with, from Elizabeth Taylor and Richard Burton to Eminem and Kimberly Scott. Whilst Trump and O'Donnell's relationship is currently private, should it ever be revealed it will go down in history as being one of the greatest love stories of all time. Provided Trump does not have the Secret Service kill her first.

Chapter Ten

The Vice President

'He wants to hang all gay people.'
- Donald Trump, 17 October 2017,
on Vice President Mike Pence.

During the presidential election, candidates are expected to announce their running mate. This person then forms a 'joint-ticket' with the main candidate, as voters are shown who will replace the president in the event of a death or resignation. Every selection is based on strategy. Candidates will usually appoint a vice presidential running mate to tap into a demographic that they themselves cannot.

For example, Barack Obama chose Joe Biden to be his running mate as an old, white man would settle concerns from some voters that America was not ready for a black president. Bill Clinton chose Al Gore to settle concerns from some voters that America did not need another old, white male president.

Hillary Clinton chose her running mate to be Senator Tim Kaine, mainly because he was fluent in Spanish. By appointing Kaine, Hillary hoped to obtain more Hispanic voters and help with securing the state of Virginia, Kaine's home state.

Further, Hillary did not need to be concerned that her running mate would eclipse her. In his own words, 'I'm boring. But boring is the fastest growing demographic in the country.'

Trump faced a difficult choice in selecting a running mate. Firstly, the majority of Republican stalwarts had publicly opposed him, thinking that his victory would be unlikely. Once it became clear that Trump would defeat the other Republican nominees, the tone used by senior Republicans quickly changed. However, Trump is not one to forgive nor forget.

Some advisers recommended to Trump that he should select an uncontroversial figure. Someone with a safe pair of hands, to alleviate any concerns within the public that Trump was too unpredictable.

Shawn Mendes prepared a list for Trump to consider. On this list were New Jersey Governor Chris Christie, former House Speaker Newt Gingrich and Indiana Governor Mike Pence.

Trump pretended to consider the list, but his mind was already made up. Newt Gingrich sounded like a character from *Harry Potter*, and those movies scared him. Chris Christie was a funny name, but if he said it ten times fast he would become tongue tied. Mike Pence it was.

So who was this snow white haired man from Indiana?

Michael (Mike) Pence was born on 8 June 1959 in Columbus, Indiana. He had a relatively simple childhood and would later study history at Hanover College. During this time, he was a Democrat voter. He then studied law at the Indiana University and began to vote Republican, after watching with fascination Ronald Reagan at work.

Once he graduated from law school, he went into private practice for seven years. Afterwards, he left the show to host a radio program called '*The Mike Pence Show*'. This was a mildly conservative program.

In 2001, he commenced his political career by winning a seat in the House of Representatives for Indiana. Then, from 2013 to 2017 he served as Indiana's Governor.

Financially, he was not the best governor. He inherited a two billion dollar budget surplus, but he was unable to boost Indiana's economic growth above the national average. However, he was able to incorporate fiscal responsibility by ensuring the state maintained its AAA credit rating.

A strong coal supporter, Pence did not believe in climate change and resisted all of Obama's attempts at reducing emissions. In 2016, Pence publicly stated that under no circumstance would Indiana ever consider reducing emissions.

Pence was also a strong NRA supporter. He legalised firearms being kept in vehicles on school property and recruited the NRA to train the National Guard on concealed carry. This was considered controversial as the NRA is a civilian organisation and the National Guard is military. Further, Pence reduced the liability of gun and ammunition manufacturers so they could not be sued for illegal sale of weapons.

He is most well known for introducing a bill into Indiana that legalised discrimination against the LGBT on religious grounds. The bill received widespread condemnation which caused Pence to revise it. Predictably, he is strongly anti-abortion.

To put it mildly, Pence was the perfect conservative candidate to attract religious voters to Trump's team. He was an effective administrator who was believed to add some stability to the often-changing Trump side.

There was just one problem - Pence was a big supporter of Senator Ted Cruz. During the 2016 Republican primaries, Pence endorsed Cruz as his preferred candidate. He went on the record to say that Cruz would make a better president than Trump.

At the time of his endorsement, Shawn was left flummoxed. He had proposed Pence to Trump as a running mate, but the man was endorsing his rival. Notwithstanding that at the time of endorsement Cruz was dead and had been replaced with a robot, it presented a big hurdle for Shawn to overcome.

Trump himself was furious. He viewed it as an attack on his character and told Shawn that under no circumstances would Pence ever be allowed to become his running mate. He was a traitor and could not be trusted.

Shawn had to use every manipulative skill he possessed to convince Trump that Pence would be the best running mate. Pence had links to the wealthy Koch family. Their support during the election would be necessary if they were to rival the Clinton war chest. Reluctantly, Trump agreed with Shawn. He would rather spend somebody else's money than his own.

Approaches were made to Pence from Trump's camp to see if he would be interested in becoming the running mate. Pence refused. The man was ambitious and wanted to become president one day himself. He did not want to stop at the office of vice presidency, like so many before him. By allying himself with Trump, he would forever be tainted by the man. Pence took the view that Trump's popularity would die over time and that all of his Cabinet ministers would be left in the same boat.

Shawn knew that Trump needed Pence if they were going to succeed, but the man was not prepared to sign up. The only way that this would occur would be via the old fashioned method of blackmail. Shawn needed to find some dirt on Pence.

Using his Russian contacts via Island Records, hackers penetrated Pence's computer and discovered a startling secret that many supporters of Pence would be shocked to hear. Pence was gluten-intolerant.

At first, Shawn did not believe the hackers when they provided this information. There was no way that the Governor of Indiana could be allergic to gluten. The man was a leading conservative. This would completely destroy his support base.

The evidence proved right. Pence's bank statements showed that he only ever bought food that did not contain gluten. He was also a subscriber to the magazine '*Living Without Gluten*'.

Shawn took this revelation directly to Pence on 14 July 2016. Pence begged Shawn not to reveal to the world that he was gluten-intolerant, promising to do anything in return if he kept the information private.

The following day, Trump announced on Twitter that Pence would be his running mate.

Throughout the campaign, Pence remained completely loyal to Trump, no matter what Trump said or did. This can only be explained by Pence's fear about his gluten secret being revealed.

On the day of the announcement, Pence said that he was 'very supportive of Donald Trump's call to temporarily suspend immigration from countries where terrorist influence and impact represents a threat to the United States.' He further said that he was fully supportive of building a wall between the USA and Mexico. The basis of his support of the wall was that Shawn told Pence that if Corden was allowed to defeat Trump, his secret would be revealed.

Pence continued to support Trump and on 8 November 2016, he was elected Vice President of the United States. Knowing that he could trust him given the blackmail material they had on him, Trump appointed Pence as the chairman of the transition phase. Pence was charged with preparing lists of names for Trump's cabinet, that would be provided to Shawn before being sent to Trump.

Pence's influence grew during this time, as many wary Republicans would go to Pence to seek reassurance about Trump's policies. There were still many within the party concerned about the inclinations of their new leader.

When Pence was sworn in as Vice President, he chose for the Bible to be open at a certain passage. The passage, opened to 2 Chronicles 7:14 reads:

> *'If my people, which are called by my name, shall humble them-selves, and pray, and seek my face, and turn from their wicked ways; then will I hear from heaven, and will forgive their sin, and will heal their land.'*

Many believed this passage to relate to Pence's religious leanings. However, it is a prayer from Pence that no one will ever learn of his gluten intolerance.

Like all vice presidents before him, Pence has not really done anything in the role. He has attended events and cut ribbons, but his position is there as a ceremonial one. Waiting in the wings, in case any ill should befall the President, is his only duty.

There are many Democrat voters out there who are more con-cerned by Pence than they are by Trump. They view Pence as the more dangerous of the two. Whereas Trump may be unpredictable, Pence holds conservative views and is efficient. If he were to ever be President, he would be able to pass many of his views into law. This could be devastating for Obama's legacy.

Interestingly, there is a fear that as Shawn becomes more politically savvy, he may realise that he no longer needs Trump as his puppet. Whereas Shawn needs to manipulate Trump into taking on his view, with Pence he simply needs to blackmail him using the gluten material.

Pence could prove to be a more pliable President that is more easily controlled. However, the biggest hurdle Pence faces of ever being

President is that he is now a Trump man through and through. Should Trump prove to be an unpopular president, the polls will slip and Pence will become unelectable.

Even though Shawn knows that he can control Pence, this would be pointless if Pence cannot win the 2020 election. For now, it is highly likely that Shawn will simply wait to see how the polls shape up in the lead up to 2020, before deciding on which candidate should run.

In March 2017, Mike Pence hurt his chances of ever being considered as a presidential-nominee by Shawn when he accidentally said in public that he refuses to dine alone with any woman other than his wife. This included foreign diplomats and high ranking women, as he did not trust them to act appropriately around him.

The real reason why he refuses to dine alone with them? Pence knows that women are savvy and did not want any of them realising that his food were all gluten-free choices. Being a firm believer that all women are gossips, Pence feared they would then go to the press with his secret.

When this revelation was made, all female voters in the country despaired. There was not a single woman in the country, with the exception of Rosie O'Donnell who is madly in love with Trump, who did not dream about Pence. They all wanted him. And here he was, publicly saying that he was unattainable and would not dine with them alone.

After this, Pence's public support dropped. Female voters no longer wanted to see him if they could not be with him. Shawn watched this with narrowed eyes, knowing that his back-up plan for President was becoming less and less likely to succeed over time.

Readers are encouraged to watch this space, as Trump may be inclined to replace Pence at some point, under the careful prodding of Shawn. And who would be the replacement? Only time will tell.

Chapter Eleven

The Witchery of Ivanka Trump

'I've said if Ivanka weren't my daughter, perhaps I'd be dating her.'
- Donald Trump, 24 August 2006, Video Interview.

There are not many people in the world who could compete with the resume of Ivanka Trump. An author, businesswoman, fashion design, television celebrity and now adviser to the President, Ivanka has had a long and successful career. She is only currently thirty five years old, but has risen through the ranks quickly.

Along with Shawn Mendes, she is in the President's inner circle and has his ear on most matters of public policy. A strong ally of Shawn, she has been a pillar in the Trump administration to date.

Some claim that Donald Trump hates women and views them as inferior to men. This could not be further from the truth. His main security guard is a female machine called Melania and his lover, Rosie O'Donnell, is in his thoughts all the time. Additionally, his second most influential adviser is Ivanka Trump.

With her flawless looks and impeccable fashion style, she is considered to be the most powerful First Daughter in America's history. However, she is also a Satanist cult member and practices low-level witchery in order to influence the minds of her critics.

Born to Trump's first wife on 30 October 1981 in New York City, she would be raised amongst the greats, experiencing a level of wealth that most could only dream about.

Ivanka decided to follow in her father's footsteps and obtain a degree in economics at university. She attended Georgetown University and the University of Pennsylvania. Whilst her main field of study was economics, during the night she became involved in satanic cult rituals, after a fellow student lured her in. Within the space of a month, Ivanka rose to be the cult leader, specialising in dark magic.

There are some reports that J.K. Rowling, the author of the *Harry Potter* series, based the character of Bellatrix Lestrange on Ivanka Trump. Bellatrix was a beautiful witch who had a high level of skill in dark magic, before losing her looks when she was sent to the wizarding prison for crimes against humanity.

Ivanka Trump can speak French and Czech, two nations that are well known for historically being the source of magic. It is highly likely Ivanka only learnt these languages so she could read magic books that originated from these countries.

In 2005, the year that Trump married the robot Melania, Ivanka joined the family business. On the side, Ivanka set up a jewellery company and a fashion retail store. She also set up her own line of fashion.

She models regularly, having worked for Tommy Hilfiger, Sasson Jeans and the Trump Organisation. On television, she co-hosted *The Celebrity Apprentice* for one season as well as Miss Teen USA.

As an established author, Ivanka has released two books, *The Trump Card: Playing to Win in Work and Life* and *Women Who Work: Rewriting the Rules for Success*. Of course, being wealthy she did not need to write the books herself and instead hired a ghost writer to do all of the work for her, simply lending her name to the book.

In the same year that Ivanka started working for the Trump Organisation, she met Jared Kushner, a real estate developer. They dated for three years until 2008 when they broke up, because Kushner's parents did not approve of her.

The Kushner family is a well known Jewish family. They objected to the relationship on the basis that Ivanka was not Jewish and practiced witchcraft. Whilst the Satanist worshipping was not to Kushner's parents liking, the non-Jewish religion was a deal breaker.

In a startling turn of events, Ivanka decided to convert to Judaism in July 2009 in order to win Kushner back. It worked - on 25 October 2009, the two married in a Jewish ceremony. Since then, Ivanka has been a strong supporter of the Jewish community and Israel.

Together, Ivanka and Kushner are estimated to be worth over 700 million dollars, a paltry sum compared to the wealth Trump decides he has from a day to day basis.

Ivanka is also best friends with Chelsea Clinton and Paris Hilton, displaying that in the celebrity world, everybody knows everybody.

During the presidential election, Trump relied heavily upon Ivanka's advice. Trump said that she was his leading adviser on women's health and women generally. He endorsed her as being one of the greatest women that he knew.

Did Shawn Mendes object to Ivanka's influence, fearing that she would detract from his own advice? No. Shawn relished in it. Together, the two could convince Trump to do almost anything. When one of them failed to coerce Trump into adopting a policy, they would call on the other for assistance. Trump would often remark that only if they both agreed would he do something - and they both always agreed.

Shawn viewed Ivanka as the key to displaying a softer side of Trump. Whenever Trump was getting heavily blasted in the media for being anti-women or out of touch, he would roll out Ivanka to negate these fears. Ivanka herself was used in many advertisements at the behest of Shawn, hoping to get Trump to appeal to female voters.

At the 2016 Republican National Convention, Ivanka was used to introduce Trump. As she said, 'One of my father's greatest talents is the ability to see the potential in people.'

The crowd roared their approval at her speech. Was this because of her superb speech making ability? Was it because the audience agreed with what she was saying? Or was it simply because she was casting dark magic on the audience, compelling them to cheer? The latter. Wherever Ivanka went during the election, she would cast magic on the people surrounding her to ensure that they would vote for her father. This was one of the campaign's most effective tools at securing support.

Additionally, there is some speculation that Ivanka Trump led the security team that captured Carrie Fisher, before she could warn Ellen about the robot Ted Cruz and Melania. Ivanka is said to have taken Carrie and cast magic on her, placing her in a frozen state so she could be transported back to New York City and placed in storage, until such time as Trump or Shawn had use of her.

If this is true, and there is no evidence to the contrary, many *Star Wars* fans will be furious at Ivanka. Carrie Fisher is a pop culture hero and it would be viewed by these fans as unacceptable conduct in freezing her and holding her prisoner.

Once Trump was successful in securing the presidency, Ivanka stepped down from her role at the Trump Organisation and was later appointed as Adviser to the President. She takes no salary and effectively works for free, aside from the 700 hundred million dollar wealth she holds.

There has been some controversy in her appointment. In April 2017 the Chinese Government extended trademarks to Ivanka's business. On the exact same day, President Trump hosted the President of China along with Ivanka. Critics stated that Ivanka was using her government position to further her own business interests, which would amount to corruption.

However, these critics are failing to take into account Ivanka's witchery. It is not her government position that resulted in the business success, it is the fact that she cast magic on Chinese officials. Should the Chinese Government discover this, it will likely harm the relationship between the USA and China.

For now, Ivanka is playing a valuable part in the Trump administration. Shawn views her as a useful fill-in when he is not in the USA. As a pop sensation, he is required to perform concerts around the world. During this time, Ivanka takes his place as Trump's chief adviser.

Her magic can also be used to convince reluctant Republican congressmen and Senators to vote in support of Trump's initiatives. There is some speculation that she may in fact be used to convince Mexico to pay for the wall. This would be a difficult ploy, as secret-Russian President Cordén is believed to know about Ivanka's Satanist leadings and would be on the look-out for any dark magic.

But what does Ivanka herself have to gain from acting as adviser? She has always wanted to create a name for herself and get out from her father's shadow. This was why she set up her own fashion business, hoping to generate her own independent source of revenue. Obviously, she abandoned her father's religion and converted to Judaism in order to marry a wealthy man, to further expand her own assets.

There does not appear to be any logic in joining the Trump administration. Her public image is severely tarnished as she is seen as a vassal for Trump, a pretty face that he simply rolls out to show the world what his sperm created.

The answer is complicated. Ivanka has created her own wealth, yes, and she has married into a powerful family. What she lacks, however, is political connections of her own. She befriended Chelsea Clinton to get in with the Clintons, but this relationship has been destroyed following on from Shawn being fired by Hillary and instead working for Trump.

Ivanka knew that the only way she could create political connections of her own was to go work for her father in Washington D.C. Here, politicians would come to her, knowing she had the President's ear. She could promise them favours, provided that in the future they would reciprocate.

Whilst she has a bank-worthy amount of money, she now also has a bank of favours that is ever growing. Republicans and Democrats alike owe her much. Using this, if Ivanka Trump ever wanted to nominate for the presidency herself... Well, she could potentially be America's first ever female president.

Shawn realises this. Whilst close with Ivanka, he would not trust her to be President. Her magic makes her powerful and difficult to control. He would not be able to use her like he does with Trump and Pence. She could potentially be an independent President making decisions on her own - the first time in history this has ever occurred.

At the moment, this potential future has not caused a rift between Ivanka and Shawn. The two are as close as they have ever been. In time, however, when Trump's term begins to come to an end, and candidates are touted for the next Republican nomination, there could be an issue. Ivanka may have her name thrown in there.

Trump himself would like nothing better than creating a legacy. He has shown this in the habit of naming buildings after his family name and wanting to be remembered in the history books. If Ivanka approached him with the idea of becoming the next Republican candidate, or even his running mate should he choose to run again, Trump would be tempted.

His daughter is his most trusted child. He believes that she is the most likely to continue on the family name. It would not be out of the norm if Trump himself has already planned her succession, unbeknownst to both Ivanka and Shawn.

What would Shawn do if such a scenario arose? This is a grey area that not even your correspondent knows the answer to. Shawn now has a taste of power and would not want to lose it, least of all to a Satanist. Could he potentially have Ivanka disposed of? Is it even possible to dispose of a witch, or are they immortal? Do eight year fixed terms apply to immortals, or just humans?

Whilst we may not yet know the answer to these questions, it is worth noting that Ivanka will do anything to get what she wants. She changed religion to get the man of her dreams. She used her family to get into the business world. She used her magic to secure deals with the Chinese. What would she do to become the next President of the United States? Absolutely anything.

Chapter Twelve

From Facebook to Trumpbook

'My use of social media is not presidential
- it's MODERN DAY PRESIDENTIAL. Make America Great Again!'
- Donald Trump, 1 July 2017, Twitter.

Facebook is one of the world's cleverest organisations. Constantly adapting and evolving, Facebook has secured its spot as a top tech company.

Launched in 2004, the social media platform was originally for exclusive use by Harvard students. It was then expanded to other universities and by 2006 was open to all.

In 2012, Facebook was launched onto the stock market to much fanfare. Facebook derives its income through advertising streams and by selling research on users.

The unique feature of Facebook is the algorithm it utilises. Originally, Facebook had an EdgeRank system in place. This would affect what posts people saw on the site. The EdgeRank system was made up of three factors - weight, affinity, and time decay.

Weight was how many other people had engaged with a status. The more comments a status attracted, the more likely it would appear in a person's page.

Affinity was the closeness of the source of the status. If it was a family member or a close friend, the more likely it would appear in a person's page.

Time decay was how long ago the status was posted. A status from five minutes ago was more likely to appear on a person's page than one from three days ago.

However, Facebook was experiencing a negative backlash from users. People were complaining that they were seeing posts that they did not want to see and that Facebook was filled with irrelevant spam.

Facebook needed to adapt or it would go the same way as MySpace, into the dark corners of the Internet where only the depraved would visit.

In order to improve users' experiences, Facebook needed to learn what their preferences were. What did they want to see more of? What did they want to see less of? But Facebook knew that it could not send out an email to all users asking them to fill in a survey. People hate being asked what to do and few people would fill it out.

So Facebook decided to invent the 'like' button. People would 'like' statuses, photos, comments and videos which would then send a signal to Facebook on their preferences.

Using this, Facebook then created the Facebook Algorithm. This was a clever piece of computer coding that, along with one hundred thousand other factors, would assess a person and determine what needed to appear in their News Feed.

The other factors that Facebook would take into account would be how long a person spent reading a status, whether they engaged with the status, whether they watched a video for the full length, whether they expanded the video, and whether they turned sound on. Basically, Facebook tracked and observed everything, using this research to provide the best experience humanly possible.

Because of this high level research, Facebook's advertising platform is the best in the world. Companies can create an account with Facebook and target an advertisement as specifically as they want. A wedding gift company can target people whose close friends recently became engaged. A bank can target people suffering from poor finance. A pharmaceutical company can target people suffering from mental issues.

Accordingly, most companies have moved onto Facebook advertising. The platform is simply too effective to not use. Politicians have also cottoned on to this social media giant. Whereas previously they would engage in solid doorknocking and telemarketing exercises, now for a few thousand dollars they can have an advertisement placed in front of every single resident of their electorate, within a few seconds.

Both Donald Trump and Hillary Clinton took advantage of Facebook during the election campaign. Hillary had been advised by Shawn Mendes during 2013 and learnt all about the benefits of social media. Under the watchful supervision of Shawn, a social media team had been set up for her campaign. Even though she did not have the benefit of Shawn's advice during the actual election campaign, she still remembered the lessons he had taught her and used them to good effect.

Trump had an even better advantage. He had Shawn during the election campaign. This allowed him to constantly adjust to Facebook's changes with the Algorithm and permitted him to target his advertisements to swinging voters.

Still, this was not enough. Both the Trump and Clinton camps were injecting equal amounts into Facebook advertising. Their ads were appearing before swinging voters only to have little impact. A swinging voter would see a pro-Trump ad, and then ten minutes later would see a pro-Hillary ad. This did not help them make up their mind in the slightest.

Shawn knew that something needed to be done. He was initially brought into Trump's team because of his social media influence and his ability to use social media platforms to gain huge followings. But here he was, being beaten by the social media team he himself had set up. If he did not perform, Trump could turn on him and dismiss him as an adviser.

This he could not allow. Trump was the sole reason he had been signed up with Island Records. If Trump dismissed him, that could possibly also extend to him being dismissed as a musician. His entire career would be over.

Trump needed to dominate on social media. Not only did users' Facebook accounts need to be covered in pro-Trump content, it also needed to contain solid anti-Hillary material. However, this could not be overly obvious. The manipulation needed to be so subtle that the average user would not realise what was going on. Any news articles that contained negative Hillary stories, even ones from independent news stations, needed to appear in the Newsfeed. Likewise, any articles that were pro-Trump also needed to use the Algorithm to their advantage and appear.

Shawn decided in early 2016 that the best way would be a two-pronged approach. For the first part of his plan, he involved Ivanka Trump, the converted Jew.

Conveniently enough, the creator of Facebook, Mark Zuckerberg, was also a Jew. Just like all Canadians know each other and can secretly communicate, so can the Jews.

Ivanka flew to Palo Alto, California, where Zuckerberg lives. Naturally, Zuckerberg accepted her invitation to dine at a local Chinese restaurant. He was curious as to why the daughter of a presidential candidate wanted to visit him. He assumed that the reason was to get a greater understanding of Facebook advertising. Zuckerberg was only too happy to meet with a Trump, who he thought would spend millions in Facebook advertising.

Within minutes of meeting, Ivanka cast a spell on Zuckerberg, convincing him to add two factors to the one hundred thousand factor Algorithm.

What were these mysterious factors added to Facebook? One was an anti-Clinton factor. Any Clinton status, photo or video that appeared in Facebook containing a pro-Clinton leaning would receive a negative impact under the Algorithm. The same was true for any anti-Clinton material.

The second factor was the Trump factor. Any pro-Trump material would receive a boost whilst any anti-Trump material would be negatively received.

Note the genius of Shawn's plan here. He did not block any pro-Clinton material. Nor did he flood the system with pro-Trump material. He merely added in two factors to the Algorithm. Pro-Clinton material would still appear, it would just be less prominent than before. The change would not be noticed by anyone, but over time it would impact on the population and swinging voters.

Shawn was not finished with his plan. The second part of his plan was to involve Trump's Russian allies. There needed to be an injection of Facebook advertising that would not be tracked by American authorities. The source needed to be outside of America so it could never be traced back to Trump.

The Russian oligarchs agreed immediately. They were eager to see their man appointed as President. Together, they combined their funds and over the time of the election a steady stream of high quality Facebook ads were appearing.

His plan working, Shawn began to revel in the social media dominance Trump was having over Hillary. The side effects of the plan were resulting in additional free coverage. Nearly everybody posted a Facebook status about Trump, feeling compelled by the subtle advertising they were experiencing. Those who hated Trump posted such negative statuses that they alienated their Facebook friends and made the ones leaning towards Trump even more likely to vote for him.

Those who loved Trump posted positive statuses and made their friends realise that they too could vote for him without fear of repercussion.

The two aspects to his plan set in motion, Shawn set up one final push on social media. He decided to launch a concept that Trump would later dub 'Fake News'. Fake News was the perfect solution to the problem facing the Trump campaign - every time Trump said something controversial, local media would jump on it and make it their story of the day. Over time, this could sway voters against the Trump camp as they saw negative news stories on television night after night. No matter what appeared on Facebook, they would not be able to be converted.

Shawn set up a team within the Trump campaign. This team would be granted the coveted name of Covfefe, named after the joint-operation of Trump and Shawn. Team Covfefe would be responsible for creating ludicrous stories on Trump.

For example, they widely published stories that Trump had previously been personally bankrupt. This was not true. Whilst Trump's companies had, at times, declared bankruptcy, Trump himself never had.

What was the purpose behind creating Fake News? Well, these fake stories would be quickly spread across social media. People would assume them to be true. Once enough people had seen the fake stories, the Trump campaign would release a statement that discredited the story and provide clear facts in support. In this way, any of Trump's supporters seeing a negative story on Trump would suddenly label it as Fake News, even if it was true.

Team Covfefe essentially silenced all of Trump's critics. Any legitimate negative story on him was ignored by his supporters and swinging voters could no longer trust the source. Suddenly, Trump's rhetoric on the media being biased and favouring the establishment seemed true.

Never before in the history of American politics had a campaign used social media in such an effective way. Whereas previously Obama had used Facebook to inspire, Trump now used it to instil fear.

A member of Team Covfefe, who was dismissed shortly after the election, provided the following statement to your correspondent:

> 'We worked across the clock. Basically, Trump wanted as many stories out there as possible about him. No matter how ridiculous, we had to write it and get it out. The more stories that we generated, the bigger the Fake News phenomenon became. Sometimes we thought we were getting way too ridiculous. Surely someone should have found out what we were doing. But nope, everyone kept believing it. At one point, we wrote a story that Trump was planning on getting all manufacturing jobs back in America. It was crazy. No one could do that without suddenly banning imports and destroying our relationship with all other countries. But everyone believed it when we published it. The story actually became a good news story and Trump's support increased… So even though it was Fake News, Trump decided to adopt it as one of his core policies. We all laughed about it at the time.'

After the election, Facebook suffered from criticism that it had allowed Fake News to permeate the online platform. Currently, the organisation is subject to a congressional investigation that is looking into Russian influence during the campaign.

Some readers may question why Facebook has not disclosed what occurred during the campaign. However, it is likely that Zuckerberg is still under the influence of Ivanka Trump. With her magic in place, there is no possibility that Facebook will provide any evidence that will work against President Trump.

Chapter Thirteen

All Life Needs is a Bit of Spice

'We are going to have an unbelievable, perhaps record-setting turnout for the inauguration, and there will be plenty of movie and entertainment stars. All the dress shops are sold out in Washington.
It's hard to find a great dress for this inauguration.'
- Donald Trump, 9 January 2017, New York Times Interview.

Under the careful guidance of Shawn Mendes, Trump's campaign was building momentum. Hillary, who had enjoyed social media dominance for so long after being tutored by Shawn, was suddenly at a disadvantage with the two-pronged approach by the Trump camp. The AWJL was failing to have an impact and President Obama was steadily losing popularity. The robot Ted Cruz was being rolled out when needed and any voices of dissent were quickly tarnished with being establishment figures and of endorsing the rise of Fake News.

Suddenly, what had seemed so impossible only months before, became a potential reality. In March 2016, people from around the world were suddenly asking - could Donald Trump win the Presidency of the United States?

Of course not, most people comforted themselves by saying. No way would America ever elect the man. Hillary was a guaranteed winner. The USA would have their first female president and once again would they be ruled by a Clinton.

As the deniers continued to deny, Shawn looked to the future. After the election victory, many members of the press, who had previously opined that Trump could never win, were now criticising the administration for not preparing for victory. Journalists claimed that Trump himself never thought he would win and as a result he had not prepared any appointments to key positions before taking office.

Nothing could be further from the truth. In the lead up to the election, Shawn could see that Trump would win comfortably. As a result, he prepared numerous lists for Trump to consider for key appointments.

Trump was a 24/7 news source. He would tweet at all hours of the day. From his hatred or love of Rosie O'Donnell to his anger at the new host of *Celebrity Apprentice*, no one could anticipate what he would post next. Trump singlehandedly saved Twitter from becoming irrelevant.

This presented a problem to Trump's team. By never being able to predict what he would say next, it was difficult to create a narrative for the administration. What message would they sell that day? They could never answer this question. Trump would change the message every five minutes, rendering any preparation completely useless.

Shawn needed to find a flexible individual who could manipulate the truth and create a steady narrative that the media would buy. Failing which, he needed to find a complete idiot and so make Trump look like an absolute genius in comparison. Shawn settled on the latter option.

Sean Spicer was born on 23 September 1971 in New York. The son of an insurance agent, he would later develop a passion for politics in high school. Studying Arts at Connecticut College, he found that he hated the press when the student paper wrote a paper and named him 'Sean Sphincter'. This was not his surname. Spicer was outraged.

Later, in 2012 he would receive a Master's degree in National Security and Strategic Studies. However, it is noted that at this time he was an influential career politician.

His life would be spent in government positions. He worked on political campaigns, he was a public affairs officer for the United States Navy Reserve, served as the communications director on the House Government Reform, performed a stint as the communications director for the Republican Conference of the US House of Representatives, and once dressed up as Easter Bunny for children.

From 2011 onwards, Spicer served as the communications director for the Republican National Committee. His main achievement during this time was to greatly expand its social media operations in order to boost the reach of the Republican Party. It was at this point that he attracted the attention of Shawn, who during this time was out of politics and building up his own social media profile. Shawn admired the zeal of an older man who understood the power of social media. He would later follow his career with interest.

There was one issue with Shawn wanting to recruit Spicer to the Trump team - Spicer was no fan of Trump, having gone on the record to criticise Trump's immigration policy.

Again, Shawn had to manipulate Trump into accepting a person who despised him, just as he did with Mike Pence. Trump could not stand people who could not stand him. It was a vicious circle. With a memory like an elephant, if any person said a single negative comment about him, that person would be forever blacklisted.

Trump was highly resistant to approaching Spicer, viewing the man as an establishment figure who the public would hate. Shawn considered requesting Ivanka's assistance in convincing her father, but he knew that if he relied on her too heavily she would become far too powerful. Instead, Shawn tried cool, hard logic with Trump.

When that failed, he told Trump that Rosie O'Donnell hated Spicer. At the time, Trump and O'Donnell were having another lover's spat. Trump immediately told Shawn that he was to recruit Spicer no matter the cost.

On 21 December 2016, Shawn approached Spicer with the job offer. Spicer accepted immediately. The following day, it was announced that Spicer would act as the press secretary for Trump, and later as the communications director.

The news was met with some surprise by Washington's journalists. Why would Spicer accept this nomination? He had publicly slammed Trump and was viewed as one of his opponents. What would he possibly have to gain by becoming the spokesman for a man he hated?

There is no simple explanation for this, as Spicer's reasons remain his own. Given that Spicer is currently residing in Antarctica to study the mating rituals of penguins, he has been unavailable for comment. However, his wife, Rebecca Miller, who oddly goes by the name of Sean Spicer, agreed to be interviewed by your correspondent. Her only condition? That her husband be given a free copy of this book.

Rebecca told your correspondent the following:

RM: Oh, Sean called me right away when he was approached with the job offer. He was over the moon. I frowned straight away. "Why do you want to work for Trump?" It did not make any sense to me at all. Sean always went on about how terrible Trump was for the Republicans. Sean worked in social media for the Republicans before taking on the role, so he could easily see the backlash Trump was receiving online. He just told me that it was a good opportunity and he was not going to give it up. Besides, it was good money and it would help pay for our children to go to college. I was still really hesitant. Lots of people were talking about Trump being assassinated and I was scared that Sean would somehow be drawn into it all. I told him that if he took up the job, he was not to take his work home under any circumstance. It would be too dangerous for the children. Oh, but he took it anyway of course. I could never stop him from doing anything that he wanted to.

JB: So why do you think he took on the role, if he could not stand Trump?

RM: He's always been really ambitious. Ever since I met him, he wanted to advance in politics. He wanted people to know his name. He wanted to be president himself one day. Imagine that, me as First Lady! Well, I never. This was a way for him to get front and centre in front of everyone. Well, I guess it worked in a way. Most people do know his name now!

Spicer would prove to be exactly the Press Secretary that Shawn Mendes wanted. Somehow, this college-educated man would make Trump appear to be a literal genius. No one would be able to claim that Spicer was more intelligent than Trump.

On 20 January 2017, President Trump was sworn into office. It was noted by the press that the crowds were less than that at Obama's first inauguration.

Spicer immediately went on the attack. He told the press that Trump had, 'the largest audience to ever to witness an inauguration, period - both in person and around the world.' He then went on to claim that the press had manipulated the camera images from the day to reduce the size of the crowd and that the floor covering the grass had minimised its impact. As soon as he made the statement, Spicer stormed out of the room, refusing to take any questions.

Some members of the press reported that Trump had told Spicer to make this statement, having been furious at the stories being run on his inauguration. This was not true. Trump never instructed Spicer to say anything. As part of Shawn's plan, Spicer would be left to his own devices. His press conferences would distract from Trump and result in the American public turning on Spicer, instead of Trump. He was to become a literal and metaphorical scapegoat.

Kellyanne Conway, who will be discussed later, leapt to Spicer's defence, the only member of the Trump administration to do so. Conway stated that Spicer could not be called a liar for making a false statement, as he was simply reporting on 'alternative facts'. Apparently Conway had read the book *1984* the night before and learnt of double-speak, a term used to confuse crowds by coining new terms and language that mean two things at once. Essentially, she was stating that there can be two facts that are completely opposite.

Two days later, Spicer held another press conference in which he changed his earlier version of events to also include people who watched the inauguration on television. He was now arguing that Trump had a higher attendance of people, using the numbers who physically attended and watched it online, compared to Obama, using just the numbers of people who physically attended. To Shawn's surprise, Spicer had actually make a correct statement, albeit based on twisted figures.

In early February, it began to be reported that Trump was angry with Spicer's performance and blamed his chief of staff for recommending the man. This was partly true. Trump was not impressed with the press coverage Spicer was obtaining and did blame his 'chief of staff'. However, this was not his official chief of staff, but rather Shawn Mendes, his primary adviser and most trusted confidante.

Trump began to get irritated, feeling that Spicer was taking away from his own press time. Shawn tried to reason with Trump, saying Spicer was taking the heat from the public which gave Trump free reign. Trump would not buy this argument and started to demand that Spicer be sacked. Shawn resisted, for a time.

On 11 April 2017, Spicer slammed Russia for supporting the Syrian government which had recently used chemical weapons. Spicer stated, 'You had someone as despicable as Hitler who didn't even sink to using chemical weapons.'

Unfortunately for Spicer, Hitler had used chemical weapons in the gas chambers and this comment was not well received by the Jewish community. There were widespread calls for his resignation, including private doubts from Trump's Jewish daughter, Ivanka. Suddenly Shawn found himself on the outer, by continuing to support Spicer's appointment.

Spicer's behaviour became increasingly erratic as time passed. When Melissa McCarthy imitated him as part of a sketch, he became the joke of a nation. A woman did a better job of being Spicer than Spicer did himself. Whenever he walked the corridors of the White House, people would snigger openly at him. Spicer fell into a deep depression.

Still, Shawn persisted with defending the man. As long as Spicer was the butt of jokes, this prevented Trump from being mocked. It is always helpful for leading politicians to have colleagues who are more embarrassing. This distracts the public and provides for a sacrificial lamb in emergency situations. Should one of Trump's policies fail spectacularly, the blame could then be placed on Spicer. No one would question it as they would all want to blame Spicer themselves.

Feeling aggrieved by certain media channels such as *The New York Times* and *CNN,* Spicer decided to ban them from his briefings. This extremist-type move was met with dismay by most, who viewed it as an affront against the ideals of free press. Trump himself did not approve the move. He liked being on media and felt that Spicer was attempting to block him from appearing on the news, in an attempt by Spicer to potentially run against him in 2020.

On 21 July 2017, Trump summoned Spicer to the Oval Office. Shawn was not informed of this meeting. With Ivanka by his side, and Melania guarding the door, he sat Spicer down on the couch and offered him a tea.

When Trump told Spicer that he would no longer need his services, Spicer openly wept, devastated by the dismissal. His entire plans were gone.

Rebecca told me:

> 'Sean did not call me that day. His phone was switched off for three days after. I saw that he had resigned on the news that night and knew something was instantly wrong. Sean would never voluntarily go. He loved speaking to the press. I knew at once that Trump must have fired him. When he finally did call me, all the passion in his voice was gone. He sounded dead. I was secretly relieved, to tell you the truth. Everyone was mocking him and he had lost all respect with the press. This was not the way for him to achieve his dreams. He could not see that at the time. I hope he does now. I really hope he does.'

Spicer did not return to his wife, preferring the company of solitude and whisky. He stayed in a cheap motel in Washington, hoping that Trump would change his mind and call him back. Surely Trump would want him again, when he realised all he did for the administration?

Unfortunately the call was not to come. He was no longer needed at the White House. Nor did any other Republican office require his services, after he had been tainted by the Trump brush. His political career over, Spicer spent night after night trying to work out what he could do.

He considered a career in comedy. After all, the comedy shows had loved him and regularly made reference to him. If he was popular there, how could he not succeed?

In the 2017 Emmys he made an appearance, where he said, 'This will be the largest audience to ever witness the Emmys, period - both in person and around the globe.' The crowd laughed, thinking that he was joking. He was just stating an alternative fact.

His career in comedy having been short-lived, Spicer once again tried to decide what the future held for him. He could not return to his wife - he had promised her that she would become First Lady. That was now impossible. He could no longer look her in the eyes without feeling shame.

On 10 October 2017, as he watching the *Nature Planet*, a segment appeared on penguins. Spicer watched the program in awe. The penguins did not judge. They did not laugh. And they did not question one another's facts. They simple were penguins. He was fascinated.

Four hours later, Spicer booked a one way ticket to Antarctica and has since studied penguins in preparation for his memoir - *Sean Spicer: What The White House Can Learn From Penguins*.

Spicer's departure from the Trump team would have a long term impact. For the first time in history, Trump had made a move against Shawn's wishes. Worse than that, he failed to consult with Shawn before doing so, preferring Ivanka's advice to that of the pop star's.

Trump received a small boost in the polls after the resignation, which made him feel vindicated by the decision. He suspected that Shawn had his own reasons for keeping Spicer around. Was Shawn potentially playing a double-game? Had he ever really left the service or Hillary? Could he be trusted?

Trump did not want to think these thoughts. He had, after all, made Shawn into the pop sensation that he is today. Shawn owed everything to Trump and had proved to be a valuable ally.

However, the office of presidency does many things to a man. For those who do not dye their hair or wear a wig, it turns hair grey. And it also makes the officeholder incredibly paranoid. They begin seeing enemies everywhere. Perhaps their long-time lover is not as faithful as she claims. Perhaps their robot wife could be hacked into by Russian oligarchs who decide to back someone else. And perhaps a pop sensation may no longer prove to be the best adviser possible.

After Spicer allegedly resigned, Shawn decided to not confront Trump about it. Furious as he was, he did not believe that there was anything to be gained by having an argument over a trifling matter. He would save his battles for another day. He could not see any purpose behind discussing it. The resignation had already occurred and could not be reversed.

Lastly, some readers may wonder whether Trump asked Rosie O'Donnell about her hatred of Spicer. It would make sense for the two lovers to discuss this, given Trump's tempering feelings on the man. If they did discuss the matter, and O'Donnell revealed that she never said anything about disliking him, this would have made Trump even more suspicious of Shawn.

O'Donnell herself had no allegiance whatsoever to Shawn Mendes. It is even doubtful that she knew of Shawn's existence. There would have been no reason for O'Donnell to lie for a man she had not met, nor for a plot she did not know about. O'Donnell would have told the truth straight away and Trump would have realised that he had been deceived and used.

And if there is one thing certain about Trump, it is that he does not forget. Nor forgive.

Chapter Fourteen

The Quadruple Agent

*'Happy New Year to all, including to my many enemies and those who
have fought me and lost so badly they just don't know what to do. Love!'*
- Donald Trump, 31 December 2016, Twitter.

In 2013, Hillary Clinton hired and fired Shawn Mendes as her adviser.
That same year, Trump himself began to prepare Mendes to take on
the role as his chief adviser. Whilst mainly significant for these events, a
further notable event was the appointment on 4 September 2013 of
James Comey as Director of the Federal Bureau of Investigation (FBI).

James Comey, born on 14 December 1960, was another New
Yorker. Of most interest, as with Trump, his father worked in real
estate. Like Hillary, he studied law. He received a Juris Doctor from
the University of Chicago Law School. His early career was that of a
criminal lawyer, where he targeted crime families and earned himself a
reputation as being a tough, but fair, prosecutor.

This reputation led him to being appointed as the Assistant US
Attorney for Virginia from 1996 to 2001 in a lengthy stint. President
George Bush noticed his talent and appointed him to be the Deputy
Attorney General on 11 December 2003.

His first task was to investigate the presidential pardon of Marc
Rich. Which president pardoned Rich? None other than President Bill
Clinton, the husband of Hillary. As early as 2003, Comey set himself
up as an enemy of the Clinton family, at least in the eyes of the public.

Also in that year, he prosecuted Martha Stewart for securities fraud. This received mixed publicity at the time. On the one hand, Stewart was a popular television figure and everybody loved her recipes. On the other hand, how the public love watching the mighty fall.

President Bush admired the aptitude and forthrightness of Comey, viewing the man as an efficient taskmaster. This opinion changed in 2004, when Comey threatened to resign if Bush continued with his push for the NSA to perform domestic wiretapping. Comey was of the opinion that wiretapping should only occur in the event that a warrant is received. Otherwise, it is illegal. This dispute eventually was fixed when President Bush and Comey had a face to face meeting. On condition that changes would be made to how the wiretapping was performed, Comey withdrew his threat to resign.

President Bush had another reason to like Comey - he was the reason that the US 'improved' their interrogation techniques, by signing off on a program to implement thirteen new measures, including waterboarding and sleep deprivation. The sleep deprivation practice that was approved allowed prisoners to be prevented from sleeping for up to 180 hours, which is the equivalent of seven and a half days. Ironically, this is also how long President Bush's naps would last for.

In 2005, Comey left government and sought work in the private sector. The Department of Defence's largest private contractor, Lockheed Martin, hired Comey as their General Counsel and Senior Vice President. He stayed in this position until 2010, when he then went to an investment management firm before then moving to the Columbia University Law School.

Needless to say, Comey had an impressive resume. From putting Martha Stewart in jail to legalising forms of torture, he had a wealth of stories that he could happily tell his two year old grandson about.

At the same time as she resigned as Secretary of State in 2013, Hillary approached Comey on the advice of Shawn Mendes. Shawn told Hillary that the man would make a valuable ally in the fights to come. He was an experienced political operator and had the unique background of working for both the private and public sector. Having worked for a defence company and having served President Bush, he would also help Hillary win over swinging voters who were not convinced that a Democrat could protect the nation.

Hillary was hesitant to contact Comey. He had been a registered Republican for his entire life and was a known Bush supporter. Further, he had investigated her husband's decision and shown the world that he was anti-Clinton. What could she possibly have to gain from allying herself with such a man?

Unlike with Trump, Hillary could be convinced into a position. She understood Shawn's argument. She knew that if she stood a chance in 2016, she would need to surround herself with people she did not like. So she called Comey and arranged to meet with him in late April of 2013.

One of Hillary's staffers at the time agreed to be interviewed by your correspondent. The staffer, who shall remain nameless, said:

> 'They met for pizza. I remember the day quite well, because Hillary wore her favourite beige pants suit but spilt coffee on it on the way there. She was freaking out about it, because for once we did not have a spare pants suit in the car. Comey was really curious about what she wanted. Everyone was speculating at the time that Hillary was going to nominate in 2016. After all, she resigned two months ago. I think a small part of Comey actually thought that she was going to ask him to be her running mate in the election.
>
> Could you imagine the scandal that would have caused? In hindsight, maybe she actually should have asked him that. I'm sure it would have stopped a lot of the issues from happening. Anyway, when she first raised her idea with Comey, he laughed, telling her that Obama would never agree. When she pressed the point, he finally relented. He wanted it bad. That much was obvious.'

Readers will be asking the question - what did Hillary suggest to Comey that he thought Obama would reject? Why did she go and see him?

Like with most questions, the answer relates to Shawn Mendes. It was his suggestion that Hillary convince Obama to take on Comey as the new FBI Director. By doing so, Hillary would have the FBI Director owing her a favour, an invaluable resource in an election.

Obama would naturally agree to the suggestion, hoping that the Clintons would later support Michelle Obama if she ever decided to nominate for the presidency. In short, it was a favour transaction all round.

In June 2013 Comey was officially nominated as the Director of the Federal Bureau of Investigation and was confirmed by the Senate on 29 July 2013 for a ten year term.

Obama may have been convinced by Hillary, but why did Comey agree to become the FBI Director under a Democrat President? Comey was a Republican and despised the Democrat Party. What game was he really playing?

At this point in time, Comey was secretly working for none other than Donald Trump as a double agent. Trump told Comey to accept the role. This would provide Trump with a key source of information close to Obama and the White House. No doubt the wiretapping efforts would help Trump understand what the public wanted and capitalise on their fears and desires. The plan was perfect. Trump had trumped both Hillary and Shawn.

It is highly unlikely that Shawn was aware of the deception at the time. He was loyal to Hillary as her adviser and would have recommended this appointment as being in her best interests. If he knew that Comey was Trump's man, he never would have suggested him.

Yet as time passed, Comey began to feel comfortable as the FBI Director. He enjoyed the position and its associated high salary. He revelled in the power of his position. Most surprisingly, he began to start to like a Democrat. Comey and Obama became friends, playing golf with each other on several occasions.

Like many Americans, Comey began to believe that Hillary would become the next US President. He did not see any chance of Trump securing victory. His wiretapping proved his theory, as in most telephone conversations he listened into, aside from people complaining about having to wait for the next *Game of Thrones* episode, they laughed about Trump. Comey started to believe that the man was nothing but a joke.

In June 2015, Trump approached his double agent and told him that he was to commence destroying the reputation of Hillary Clinton.

By this stage, Trump was the preferred Republican candidate and looked set to face off against Hillary. He wanted to annihilate her credibility to ensure that he would stroll into the White House.

Comey was concerned. If he launched a public investigation into Hillary, she would know that he was no longer her man. She would realise that she had been betrayed and any chance of continuing as FBI Director under her would be shot completely. On the other hand, if he refused, his future under Trump would be equally dubious.

He could not work out which candidate to align himself to, so he decided to turn on both. On 10 July 2015, he opened a criminal investigation into the use of Hillary's private emails. Comey's argument was that by using a private email address whilst she was Secretary of State, she had breached government protocol and potentially put the nation at risk by using an unsecured server.

This investigation would last until 5 July 2016, when the outcome of the investigation was that whilst Hillary's behaviour was careless, there was no case for her to answer to.

Readers may have been confused by this FBI investigation. During such an important time in US politics, surely an investigation into the use of a personal email account would not last for an entire year? Surely this investigation could have been concluded within the space of a week, given the abundant resources of the FBI? After all, the matter solely related to the use of a personal email account. As a federal body, the FBI would be equipped to promptly deal with a matter that allegedly affected national security.

However, Comey did not know how he wanted the investigation to end. He kept changing his mind on whether he wanted to support Hillary or Trump. On Monday, he would decide Hillary was guilty as he wanted Trump to win. On Tuesday, he would decide Hillary was innocent as he wanted Trump to lose. On Wednesday, he would want Chinese food.

In July 2016, he decided to back the Hillary camp and announced that Hillary was innocent. This was because the polls were showing that she would win the election and become President. Backing the winning horse seemed to be the best idea.

Trump was furious. He had enjoyed watching Comey regularly change his mind, as the uncertainty in the investigation only helped him. To loud cheers, he would shout to his supporters, 'Lock her up!' The saying became a catchcry amongst devout Republicans. Not only were they going to beat a Clinton at the polls, but they were going to lock one up! They had longed for this moment ever since Bill Clinton's impeachment.

Wanting Comey back as his man, Trump called Shawn. He knew that if anyone could convince Comey to come back to the Trump side, it was the pop singer.

Shawn called up Comey personally to reason with him. He set out the statistics for the man, telling him that it was clear Trump would win the election and the only way that Comey would keep his job would be if he turned on Hillary once more.

Comey, being incredibly flighty and prone to change his mind, agreed with Shawn.

On 26 October 2016, he announced that the investigation would be reopened due to new information. This was scandalous, to say the least. Here was the FBI, publicly commenting on an investigation, only thirteen days out from the election.

Surely not, all of the journalists thought when they heard the news. Could the FBI really be publicly launching an investigation into a political candidate so close to voting time? Could the FBI be attempting to influence the election for its own purposes?

Hillary was furious. For the second time, Comey had betrayed her. He had once again showed his true Republican colours. She knew that she needed the investigation to conclude quickly, or else voters would be influenced on 8 November 2016 when they went to cast their votes.

She called up Comey and sweet talked him, reassuring him she was going to win and that if he cancelled the investigation, he would keep his job.

Naturally, Comey changed his mind again. Two days out from the election, he announced, 'Based on our review, we have not changed our conclusions that we expressed in July.'

The investigation was again concluded, but it was far too late for Hillary who would lose two days later.

Was Trump angry that Comey had once again gone back to the Hillary camp? Yes and no. At first he was agitated, but after speaking to Shawn he realised that the damage was already done. When mud is thrown, some of it sticks. Swinging voters could never get the idea out of their head that she was a 'criminal', all because there was an investigation occurring that she had a Gmail account.

Hillary would later slam Comey, blaming him for her election loss. There is reason to believe Hillary's claim on this front. The polls reveal that after Comey re-launched the investigation, her support took a dive and her election winning margin disappeared. The quadruple double agent had performed his job, somehow.

Trump decided to keep Comey as FBI Director under him. Even though the man was fickle, he had been effective in destroying Hillary's support. Shawn believed that his presence would serve as a reminder to the public that Hillary was a personal email criminal and could not be trusted. Meanwhile, Trump's promise to lock her up disappeared. He was, after all, still playing golf with her husband at his golf club. That could put a damper on things.

Yet Comey was not done. He had enjoyed serving as the FBI Director under Obama. It was less stressful than his role under Bush, for he no longer had to torture anyone. Trump was a different story. The man wanted him to arrest journalists and kill off opponents. Explaining that he could not do so, at least without having time to fake it as natural causes, was exhausting on a day to day basis. No matter how many times he told Trump the reason why he could not do it, the man kept asking the same question, day after day.

Comey realised that he had backed the wrong candidate. He wanted President Clinton, not President Trump. This was a depressing turn of events for him. Only four years into a ten year term, he would have to wait at least until 2020 for a new president to appear. Even then, Trump could win again in 2020, meaning that he would be stuck with him for the entire duration of his term.

Having turned on Trump before, Comey realised that his next course of action would be to remove the man as president. He may no longer be able to serve President Clinton, but he could serve President Pence if Trump was impeached.

Comey decided to launch an investigation into Trump as part of a Russian investigation. The public response was immense. Not only had Comey investigated a presidential candidate, he was now investigating the President himself!

Clearly, Comey did not have long-term career ambitions and was looking for an early retirement. If not, the man was an idiot.

On 9 May 2017, Trump sacked Comey. Whilst Trump was criticised for this decision, this was the right call. The man had turned on every single person in Washington D.C. Before long, he would probably have launched an investigation into himself. In any event, if the FBI Director takes a whole year to investigate an email claim, he is probably not the most efficient man for the job.

Shawn backed Trump's call. The man had become too unpredictable and was no longer a worthwhile ally. Instead of reminding the public about Clinton's email indiscretions, he was now reminding the public Trump owed his allegiance to Russia, a fact that Shawn wanted to keep quiet.

Comey then slid quietly into retirement. Many asked what the man would do with his time now. For so long he had served government and private companies, holding high level and stressful roles that demanded all of his time. Would he spend his free time with his children? Would he travel the world? Would he start a winery?

This was not for Comey. He decided that he would sell his story to the highest bidder, welcoming an auction from publishers to secure his publication rights. During his time as FBI Director, he kept a diary that recorded all of his interactions with Trump. An ironic end for Comey - the man had preached the importance of keeping government information secure, to then sell it to the private industry. There is speculation that he sold his story for ten million dollars. Others believe he sold it for a magical bean.

Some readers may be wondering why the FBI did not have him killed, after he effectively agreed to leak confidential information to the public. The FBI has a duty to keep information secret and safe, and will do anything to protect it. However, Trump and Shawn took the view that the man was not intelligent enough to be able to write down anything of interest. They suspect, and various sources confirm this is the case, that what Comey believes are notes are actually just pictures he drew during meetings when bored. There is nothing of value contained within his notes.

The above criticism aside, it is important to remember Comey as a man of impeccable integrity. Here was a man, willing to betray anyone for God only knows what reason. He will go down in history as the only person to serve President Bush, then President Obama, then candidate Hillary Clinton, then Shawn Mendes, then candidate Donald Trump, then candidate Hillary Clinton, then candidate Donald Trump, then candidate Hillary Clinton, then candidate Donald Trump, then Mike Pence.

Chapter Fifteen

The Weinstein Plot

'You know, I'm automatically attracted to beautiful - I just start kissing them. It's like a magnet. Just kiss. I don't even wait. And when you're a star, they let you do it. You can do anything... Grab them by the pussy. You can do anything.'
- Donald Trump, 2005, Video Recording.

With a surname that sounds like Einstein, readers would probably have known pre-October 2017 that Harvey Weinstein was a glorified moron. Trump was no exception to this knowledge, viewing the man as being in his top five enemies list (Trump has an enemies list of over seven hundred pages, so this was quite an achievement for Weinstein).

Having produced famous films such as *Pulp Fiction* and *Clerks*, as well as producing the plays *The Producers* and *Billy Elliot the Musical*, he was a well known name within Hollywood, where everybody was more than happy to sing his praises whilst he held influence.

Following the allegations made against him in October 2017, his popularity took a turn for the worse and nearly every celebrity decided that they had always hated the man. The average member of the public did not know of his existence before then, but they too decided that the man was the embodiment of all evil and should be immediately jailed or shot.

But who was he really?

Born on 19 March 1952 in New York City, he was raised to have a passion for movies. His parents were obsessed and his brother, Bob

Weinstein, shared his love for film. Together, the two brothers set up a production company where they produced rock concerts in the 1970s. At the age of eighteen, Weinstein began to make a name for himself already.

For any of his friends, the ambition was clear in him. He wanted to succeed. And he wanted others to know that he had succeeded. He had a certain lust for power and a desire for people around him to notice when he entered a room. Using this drive, he put his career into fast mode.

Using the profits he and his brother made from the rock concerts, they set up a company called Miramax, which was named after both of their parents (Miriam and Max). The start of Miramax saw it focusing on music concert films, as opposed to commercial ones.

The 1980s then saw Miramax turn its attention towards arthouse films. Partnering with Amnesty International, Miramax produced a film called *The Secret Policeman's Other Ball* in 1982. Amnesty Internal credits Miramax with having boosted its name recognition within the US, a remarkable achievement.

Then, in the 1990s Disney wanted to purchase the film production company. Disney had noticed the success and wanted a piece of the action. The offer on the table? 80 million dollars. The Weinsteins accepted almost immediately, giving each brother the cool sum of 40 million each. Disney kept on both as the head of the company. It was then that Miramax produced *Pulp Fiction*, a cult film that has survived in popularity to this date.

On 30 September 2005, the brothers left Miramax and set up the Weinstein Company, alongside Quentin Tarantino. At this company, Weinstein would develop a reputation as being a hard taskmaster. Many within the industry criticised him for the cuts he would perform on films, believing that he was removing some of their best work from the film.

Understandably, however, Weinstein needed to cut scenes from films if they were unworkable. He was, after all, a producer and needed to turn a profit to maintain the company. He was viewed to be unnecessarily aggressive in his approach, having reportedly once put a journalist in a headlock for asking annoying questions. For those who have encountered a journalist, this could be considered reasonable and Weinstein should not be judged for this incident alone.

Despite all of the rumours that were swirling around about him, Weinstein was still loved by Hollywood. It is noted that in all Oscar acceptance speeches since 1966, Weinstein has been thanked in an equal amount to God. He is second only to Steven Spielberg.

Readers should take careful note of this position. Prior to October 2017, he was the second most popular man in Hollywood. Many actors and actresses owed their success to the man. There were few people who could match his influence and gravitas.

All of his status came to a crashing halt in October 2017 when it was reported that over a dozen women had accused him of rape, sexual harassment or assault. Following this, many celebrities came out and alleged that he had also acted inappropriately towards them.

As such, the rise of Weinstein had come to a shocking end. No one leapt to his defence and he was left alone to wallow in his own misery. A just end, for a man who had committed unspeakable acts. Or was it?

Your correspondent has unveiled shocking evidence that would indicate Weinstein had acted against Trump. It is believed that he sought to prevent Trump from ever becoming president and, as a result, he was blacklisted by the new administration and his fall was orchestrated by the Trump camp.

Ridiculous! Some readers may claim at this point. Weinstein is a pig, they would say, and deserved everything he got. There was no way that he worked against Trump. And how could Trump destroy a man of such influence anyway?

For these sceptical readers, who can be quite rude, there are a number of facts about the Weinstein matter that simply do not add up.

Firstly, the man is responsible for Amnesty International gaining a foothold in the USA. Could a person who introduced a charity to the world's most powerful country truly be evil?

Secondly, the man was incredibly popular in Hollywood. Many celebrities owed their success to him. He was thanked in numerous speeches in public.

Thirdly, and most revealing, Weinstein's fall occurred when Trump was President.

So what did Weinstein do that resulted in Trump turning his attention on him?

The year was 2016. The month was July. Trump and Hillary were close in the polls, although the majority still assumed that Hillary would win the election. People around the country were reporting that they were uninspired by the election and wished there was a candidate they could openly support.

People were ashamed to admit they were planning to vote for Trump. People were ashamed to admit that they liked Hillary's pantsuit.

Weinstein, being a man of the people who liked to deliver material that people enjoyed, saw his opportunity. What if he nominated for the presidency as an independent? What if he offered people an alternative to Trump and Hillary? Surely there would be no better chance in American history than the one that faced him. Here were two deeply unpopular candidates with an electorate that was not listening. It was almost as if it was too easy.

Yet running for president is no cheap matter. He needed financial backers. Whilst Disney had sent him 40 million dollars and his new company was turning a solid profit, this would not be enough to win over the electorate. He needed more.

Enter Hollywood. Here, the people loved him. They publicly supported him all the time. For decades now they had, without knowing, practiced their speeches to advocate for him. If he was to hold a presidential launch, he could roll out celebrity after celebrity to endorse him. Utilising all of their statuses and associated social media accounts, he could easily reach the entire electorate. Victory was all but assured.

Weinstein began to make the calls. Every single celebrity he phoned answered and agreed to endorse him. To do so, they would need to be strategic. Neither Hillary nor Trump could know what he was up to. He wanted them focused on each other. They would perform research on the other candidate and publicly smear them, allowing Weinstein to act in secret behind closed doors. By the time he came out in public, it would be too late for them to do anything.

The celebrities began by slamming Trump publicly. Hollywood turned against him, at the request of Weinstein. The man was an easier target than Hillary. He was already viewed as unpopular and Weinstein did not want to focus all of his efforts on both candidates at once. He wanted to take one out at a time. Once Hollywood had destroyed Trump's credibility, they would then aim at Hillary. When that was done, Weinstein would announce his candidacy.

It seemed to be the perfect plan. Now all that he needed was actual policies to take to the election. He had time to consider this whilst Hollywood was busy blasting Trump. This was difficult for him, as his entire life had been spent thinking about film production and film plots, not political matters. Should he announce a tax cut to Hollywood? No, that would not be well received. Should he loosen the laws surrounding sexual harassment? This could help with some male voters, but he did not view it as sufficient to win the election.

Suddenly, the ideal policy dawned on him. He would combine the film industry and the Defence Department. This was his perfect policy idea. Not only would it allow for great footage to be obtained in films, it would also help lessen the national debt. Instead of only expending money, the Defence Department would now start to turn a profit by broadcasting all of its wars. Research and development would assist in improving special effects and veterans could take on roles within the film industry.

North Korea seemed like the perfect country to test his new policy on. Immediately upon becoming president, he would declare war on the rogue nation and film every moment of it. Once the war was done, he would then turn the footage into a film and watch the tax dollars flow in.

Unfortunately for Weinstein, he was not aware that the average American war takes a tad longer than recording a film.

With a policy decided, the next step was to decide on a running mate. He needed somebody trustworthy who would also serve to attract voters that he himself could not convince. Effectively, he was after a female version of Donald Trump.

Readers would now know exactly who he chose to fulfil this role. Yes, that is right, Hillary Clinton.

This was a startling choice. Not only was Hillary Clinton a registered Democrat, but she was also running for president herself, a fact it is believed Weinstein knew already. So why would he choose to elect a running mate who was his opposition?

Weinstein's reasoning was that he was going to end up destroying Clinton in the polls. She would then decide that it would be better to serve as Vice President than nothing, and gladly accept his offer to be his running mate. Thus, by announcing her as his running mate during the campaign, she would be hamstrung from criticising him as he was technically her boss.

This illogical logic notwithstanding, Weinstein viewed his ploy as one of the greatest plot twists of all time. When this would be announced, he anticipated that audiences from around the world would gasp and then clap at the sudden change in direction. Pure genius, they would all shout loudly, before handing him an Oscar.

Life, however, is not a film, however much we want it to be. When Weinstein's people contacted Hillary with the offer, they first thought he was joking. Then Hillary observed the Hollywood crew repeatedly slam Trump and realised that perhaps the offer was legitimate.

Hillary recognised the threat immediately. Despite thinking that the man was a moron and his offer ridiculous, she realised the devastation that he could cause her campaign. He was far too influential and powerful. If Hollywood turned on her, she could start to suffer in the polls. This would not work.

She sent the Trump campaign an anonymous tip on Weinstein's plan, hoping that he would take action against him. But Trump was already in damage control over the Hollywood criticism. He and Shawn were doing everything possible on social media to mitigate the adverse results that were coming out from the celebrity-lashing.

Whilst Shawn Mendes was concerned about having Hollywood as an enemy of the Trump campaign, he did not lose that much sleep over it. By cleverly inserting Fake News into Facebook, Shawn convinced the American public that Hollywood was part of the establishment. This meant that every time a celebrity came out to voice their concern on Trump, the man would actually receive a boost in the polls. People were tuning out to what the celebrities were saying. The age of the macro-influencers was over.

Hillary was left on her own to defeat Weinstein. She had no assistance from Trump and the best political adviser in the country, Shawn Mendes, was loyal to her enemy. She needed to think quickly or Weinstein could become the next US President. This she could not allow.

Whilst she may be many things, Hillary is not a fool. She came up with a cunning plan that would foil Weinstein's plot and prevent him from ever announcing his candidacy. She began to phone up celebrities and ask for their public endorsement. They immediately assumed that she had agreed to Weinstein's request and was his running mate, so they happily appeared in her campaign ads.

In one quick move, Hillary had turned Weinstein's greatest weapon into her own. The celebrities who were publicly endorsing her could not then criticise her, or their image would be destroyed. Weinstein lost all of his leverage.

When he realised that he had been beaten by Hillary, he withdrew. His time had not come. Hillary would later laugh at her victory over him, right up until election night when she then came to a realisation herself - being Vice President may have been a better option.

But Trump does not forgive. Nor does he forget.

Weinstein had made a dangerous enemy of the man. Not only had he criticised him publicly, but he turned celebrities against him. Trump loved celebrities. And here they all were, saying that he would not be a good president. This could not go unchallenged.

There was only one option available to Trump - he would need to destroy the man and ensure that he could never rise up again. It would not be sufficient to just jail him or throw empty allegations of tax fraud against him. He wanted the man to experience what it felt like to have the entirety of Hollywood turn against him.

Calling up his Russian oligarch friends, Trump asked them to conduct research and find out what Weinstein's skeletons in the closet were. Failing that, they were to create the skeletons for Weinstein.

It is beyond the scope of this book to comment on whether the allegations against Weinstein are true or not. This is for a court of law to decide, as well as for the court of public opinion which is always both fair and just.

By August 2017, the Russians had done their work and provided Trump with a full file of allegations that could be used against the man. Trump was thrilled and immediately forwarded a copy of the file to *The New York Times*.

Sensing a great story, *The New York Times* published the allegations in October 2017. The result was immediate. All of Hollywood turned on him, with nearly every single celebrity publicly stating what a terrible person he is.

Despite having never commented on it previously, apparently most celebrities knew about the allegations beforehand and now felt compelled to speak out against him. Not only did Weinstein need to leave his business, but he needed to flee the entire industry. The second most loved man was now the most hated.

Some believe that a rogue Russian oligarch contacted Hillary in October 2017, with evidence that the allegations were all unfounded and completely made up. Hillary quickly disregarded this claim. She, after all, was happy with Weinstein's end.

If this is true, why did Weinstein not confront the media and tell his side of the story? This question is assuming that the accusations are unfounded, when it is likely that they are not. In every story, there is generally a cocktail of fact and fiction.

In any event, Weinstein at this point knew that he lost. His enemy was the President of the United States of America. Fighting back was a dangerous affair. What if Trump decided that he was not satisfied with simply destroying his career, but also wanted his death? With the loss of Director Comey at the FBI, Trump had cemented his control of the security services. Weinstein may have viewed his life as being in danger and decided to accept the punishment for losing.

Retreating into the shadows, he would complain to those friends remaining that he had been treated unfairly. Here he was, left with only 40 million dollars and no one to worship him.

Lastly, what was Shawn Mendes view of Trump's obliteration of Weinstein? Was he supportive of the move? Or did he view it as overkill, given that Trump won the election?

Some within Trump's camp have informed your correspondent that it was Shawn's idea to destroy Weinstein. Trump went to Shawn after the election with a large list of names of people he wanted to destroy. This included Rosie O'Donnell, Cher and Harvey Weinstein. The next day, Trump took O'Donnell off the list. A week later, she was back on. These amendments are continuing.

Given his passion for destroying his enemies, Shawn had already prepared a variety of options on how to proceed. Trump then selected the Russian option.

However, there are others who say that Shawn did not know of Trump's plan and this occurred without his knowledge. As readers will discover in the latter chapters of this book, it was around this time that the relationship between Shawn and Trump started to sour. Trump began to keep certain plans separate to his and Shawn's discussions.

One thing is clear. Weinstein made a move to destroy both Trump and Clinton. He failed. And he is now paying for it.

Chapter Sixteen

Bernie on the Outer

'Who can figure out the true meaning of "covfefe" ??? Enjoy!'
- Donald Trump, 31 May 2017, Twitter.

Whilst Trump managed to defeat Hillary Clinton at the 2016 election with the help of Shawn Mendes, Hillary was not always going to be his main opponent.

Before Hillary won the Democrat nomination, there was a possibility that Trump would instead face off against Bernie Sanders, an elderly gentlemen with a devout following who believed he was the answer to the country's pressing problems.

Sanders and Trump were similar in that they were both anti-establishment figures who were not overly aligned with the party they were aiming to head. They attracted support from voters who wanted a massive change in Washington, looking towards non-key political figures to shake the system up. Promising great change and offering hope that the world could be changed, these two managed to shake the established candidates to the core.

So why did Sanders fail to take the Democrat nomination? Why did he not elect to run as an independent, given his history? Is he related to Colonel Sanders, the founder of KFC?

On 8 September 1941, Sanders was born in New York City, the son of a Polish man and an American born woman who had Polish relatives. This was the third year of World War II, a war that would shape the world for decades to come. Sanders credits this time with establishing his passion for politics, as many relatives of his would perish in Poland for being Jewish.

Observant readers will notice that Sanders is the oldest out of Hillary, Trump and himself. Whilst the others were born in the aftermath of World War II, he was born during this time.

Sanders would later study political science at the University of Chicago and graduated with a bachelor of arts degree. He does not recall being a good student during this time as he found study 'boring and irrelevant'. However, he believed that true knowledge was found out in the community. Whilst at university, he joined the Young People's Socialist Leagues and was an active member of the Civil Rights Movement. He was highly proactive in social justice issues in New York and was later a staunch opponent of the Vietnam War.

As he faced being drafted, he lodged an application to be viewed as a conscientious objector in the war. Whilst his application was rejected, he was too old by that point to be drafted anyway. Given the tendency for candidates in elections to promote their military background, this would have been a key issue in the election had Sanders secured the nomination.

Sanders career before entering politics was an interesting one. He worked as a teacher, a carpenter and as a psychiatric aide. He also worked as a filmmaker, where he is believed to have developed a passion for films. It is unknown whether he supported Harvey Weinstein's bid to run for president.

In 1980, at the age of thirty one, Sanders decided to nominate for the mayoral race of Burlington, Vermont. Despite running as an independent against the Democrat incumbent, he won the election by ten votes. He would serve as mayor from 1981 to 1989 and would refer to himself as being a socialist mayor. This was a bold move, as during the 1980s the Cold War was still active, albeit in its dying stages, and socialism was not the popular word of the day. Most candidates would seek to avoid it like the plague.

He was viewed as an incredibly effective mayor who balanced the budget and advocated for issues that the public were passionate about. In 1987, he was ranked as one of America's top mayors by *US News &*

World Report. An impressive achievement, for an independent with no key political support.

In 1990, Sanders decided to make the move to the US Congress. Again, he ran as an independent and was elected as the first independent congressman to win since 1950.

He was not popular amongst his Democrat and Republican opponents in the Congress. Sanders was a champion for the common people and criticised the major parties for supporting the causes of the wealthy. Naturally, they did not appreciate this and attempted to isolate him. A small core of left-leaning Democrats were attracted to Sanders' way of thinking and happily met with him in private. In both 1991 and 2002, he voted against the use of force in Iraq, preferring for a peaceful option. However, he did vote for legislation in 2001 that is believed to be the justification for military action in Afghanistan following the September 11 attacks. Some critics of Sanders believe that he would change his position on items when he knew that the public would not support his view.

In 2005, Sanders made the move from the Congress to the Senate, nominating for the Vermont Senate seat. The Democrat Party decided to support him in this election, despite him running as an independent. As a former Vermont governor said, Sanders 'votes with the Democrats 98 percent of the time.' The Democrats wisely decided that they would not financially back another Democrat to contest the election, as Sanders popularity within the electorate all but guaranteed his victory. Even the then-Senator Barack Obama campaigned in support of Sanders.

In 2011, Sanders was viewed as the most popular Senator in the nation. His approval ratings were at 67% and his disapproval rating at 28%. Some people began to wonder whether the independent would ever consider a tilt for the White House. After all, he had gone from being Mayor to a Congressman to a Senator. What was next for the man?

Speculation grew as Sanders became more and more popular and the average American started to know who the Senator was. But would he run as an Independent? Or would he seek the Democrat nomination? There were some who strongly believed that he should run his own campaign and not be tarnished with the brush of a major party. After all, people were beginning to distrust the establishment and wanted a fresh approach.

Others believed this could not work. The major parties had immense systems in place that supported their chosen candidate. Headquarters employed advisers and key people that would ensure the campaign was run smoothly, at least from the ground level. The candidate's role was then to simply show up and perform. Administration would be handled by the experts.

But if he did decide to run as an independent, he would still be viewed as a Democrat by Republican voters anyway. Worse, he could be viewed as a dangerous socialist who was seeking to implement Soviet USA.

On 30 April 2015, Sanders announced that he would be running for the Democrat nomination. This also proved to many Republicans that the man had always been a Democrat and that his cover as an independent was a sham. This proved to many Democrats that the man had always been an independent but now wanted to coattail off their success.

When he made his announcement, he declared war on the establishment, stating, 'I don't believe that the men and women who defended American democracy fought to create a situation where billionaires own the place.' The main theme of his campaign was to support the common people, as opposed to being a mouthpiece of the billionaires.

To do so, he did not seek funding for his campaign from any wealthy donors, preferring to receive support from the average voter. Within the year, he had raised $73 million dollars, with the average donation being $27.

He was an anti-establishment figure and was beginning to gain significant support. Besides, he had a heavy presence on social media and used Twitter and Facebook to connect with voters. His dominance on social media was matched only by Trump.

So how did Sanders, as the oldest candidate, feature so heavily on the new-age social media? Why was Sanders a similar candidate to

Trump, in that they attracted voters who were sick of the establishment?

There was a common denominator for both candidates. Shawn Mendes.

Despite having been recruited by Trump, Shawn Mendes was not completely loyal to him. He was ambitious and wanted to serve as the puppet master behind the president, regardless of who it was. This is shown in how he first served Hillary Clinton, helping her become established on social media, before moving onto Trump, her main opponent, when the time suited.

Readers should note that even though Shawn was confident Trump would win the election, he did not want to place all of his eggs in one basket. He wanted to be able to have an insurance plan in place, lest his candidate fail. This insurance could not be Hillary, who had fired him and wounded his ego. It needed to be someone else. And that someone was Sanders.

Shawn was the one who convinced Sanders to nominate for the Democrat candidacy. This is why a notorious independent, who had championed staying away from the major political parties all his life, suddenly decided that he wanted to become the leader of one. There is simply no other reasonable explanation for why the career politician decided to make the shift at such a late stage.

Telling him that he needed the support of a large party, Shawn influenced Sanders into fighting Hillary for the nomination. Sanders, who had always wanted to take the top job but wanted to do so as an independent, was reluctant at first. However, his ambition overrode his principles.

Shawn then helped Sanders create his social media presence and craft his image within the election. This explains why both Sanders and Trump were similar candidates, albeit on opposite sides of the political spectrum - they were being advised by the same person.

Under the manipulative guidance of Shawn, Sanders became an immensely popular presidential candidate. He was the only one in the race to receive significant support from younger voters, who viewed his left-leaning ways as a breath of fresh air. They were eager for him to win and volunteered in droves, seeking to get the message out.

In campaign events, Sanders would draw massive crowds whilst Hillary would struggle to fill the stadiums. He was more popular amongst the voters and it was beginning to show. Polls also indicated that he would stand a stronger chance of defeating Trump than she would. Shawn's insurance policy was appearing to be effective, potentially too effective.

Trump was highly concerned about the independent-turned-Democrat candidate. The man was not part of the establishment and could not be as easily criticised as Clinton. Further, he had a grandfatherly type presence that many people respected. If Trump commenced a hate campaign against Sanders, there would be significant backlash. Could Sanders be the man to finally defeat Trump?

Shawn also became concerned. Sanders was only supposed to be a back-up plan, not the main plan. He was there to defeat Hillary, and then lose to Trump. Only in the worst case scenario was he to actually beat Trump. As he had a history of being an independent, he would be less easy to control if he became president, preferring to follow his own instincts than Shawn's. Naturally, the man needed to go. He was now a liability.

For the first time in the campaign, Shawn used his connections with the entertainment companies. Not wanting to reveal his allegiance to Trump, but needing them to assist, he called up the various heads of the television networks. One head, who shall remain nameless, told your correspondent:

> 'Shawn rang up one day out of the blue. I was pretty excited to get a call from him, as we have been wanting to host him on one of our late night shows for ages. I asked him about this at the start, and he said sure, on one condition. I said what? And he goes, well, he said that he could only do it if we did not show too much of Sanders on television. The man was old, he said, and cramped his style. Look, I didn't really read too much into it. He was a young pop singer. They all demand weird things. Justin Bieber demands a fresh puppy to towel himself off on after a shower. This request seemed pretty normal. So I complied... Yeah, I'm pretty sure the same request was made to the other networks. Strange in hindsight, I guess.'

Because of this, the major networks did not run any major stories on Sanders. For example, in December it was found that the major networks spent a total of 234 minutes reporting on Trump, but only 10 minutes on Sanders. This is despite both Sanders and Trump having polled exactly the same that month. Thanks to Shawn Mendes, the networks turned off Sanders, and it began to show in the polls.

Sanders became incredibly frustrated at the lack of media coverage. Hillary would receive hours of free advertising, whereas he would struggle to obtain even a mention. Suddenly, before the primaries had even commenced, the media was viewing Hillary as the presumptive Democrat nomination. It was widely accepted that she would win, and focus shifted to who would win the Republican nomination.

They say that it is better to be talked about badly than not at all. Nothing proves this saying more than the 2016 election. Whereas Trump was talked about badly and Sanders was not at all, Trump ended up winning the presidency, whilst Sanders was left with nothing.

Did Sanders suspect that his most trusted adviser had turned on him? Did he know that Shawn Mendes was behind him not receiving any press coverage? Did he ever think of firing Shawn and locating a new adviser, who would actually help him in the election?

No. Sanders would keep on Shawn until the very end. To this date, Sanders still believes that Shawn was loyal to him. When your correspondent contacted Sanders to request an interview for this book, he responded with:

'Who is this?'

This blanket denial proves that Sanders still does not know the truth. Nor would he want to know. It would be an embarrassing revelation that after a long-standing career, he lost because he was played by a pop star / genius.

In early 2016, Sanders would be defeated by Hillary. He watched the final votes come in from a hotel room in Los Angeles, with Shawn Mendes by his side. This would be his final election. The dream was over.

Unlike the robot Ted Cruz, Sanders was not controlled by Shawn after the election loss. Abandoning his insurance policy, Shawn left to fully dedicate himself to the Trump campaign. Sanders was left to do what he wanted.

On 12 July 2016, Sanders formally endorsed Hillary and gave speeches encouraging his own supporters to back her. He said, 'Our job is to do two things: to defeat Donald Trump and to elect Hillary Clinton… It is easy to boo, but it is harder to look your kids in the face if we are living under a Trump presidency.'

He made it his life mission, from July onwards, to ensure that Hillary was elected. He feared what the USA would be like if Trump won. Whilst Sanders had his political differences with Hillary and Barack Obama, Trump was viewed as the anti-Christ by him. There was not a single socialist bone in the man's body. Worse, he was rich.

However, just like in his own bid for the nomination, he failed to have any impact on Hillary's campaign. She would go on to lose to Trump.

In the election, 6% of the Vermont voting population wrote in Sanders name on their ballots. This was the highest amount of write-in votes in history. Even though he had been denied media coverage, he still had a strong support base. After the election, he was still found to be the most popular candidate, with a 61% approval rating compared to 43% for Trump in March 2017.

The key question is would Sanders have gone on to become President had Shawn not turned against him as an insurance policy? Would the world currently have socialist President Sanders at the helm of the world's most powerful country? Or would he still have been soundly defeated, with the combined forces of Hillary and Barack Obama turning on him?

Yes. It cannot be denied that without the actions of Shawn, Sanders would have won the election. He was the most popular candidate. He had the backing of the youth vote. And he was anti-establishment. On election day, people would have backed him and he would have soundly defeated Trump.

This would have subsequently led to Shawn's downfall. Trump is not a man to forgive. Nor does he take responsibility. Had he lost the election, he would have placed the blame squarely on Shawn and been highly vocal about it, informing the media that his chief adviser was the pop singer. This would have devastating effects.

The hypothetical President Sanders would know that he had been played and would either sideline Shawn or have him taken out. Shawn's legions of fans would no longer support him, realising that all of his songs are secret pro-Trump propaganda messages.

His entire career would be in tatters and he would be left with no allies at all. Readers may then wonder what was the point of the insurance policy at all? If Trump would turn on him in defeat, why back another candidate? This would have zero effect.

Perhaps the answer is that Shawn did not fully realise how vengeful Trump was at the start of their advisory relationship. Readers should note that at the time Shawn began his insurance policy plan, he had only been advising Trump for a short time and had not yet seen his full character. When he later realised that the man was powerful and had a strong personality, he may have revisited his earlier plan.

When Sanders does read this book, he may finally realise that the source of his defeat was Shawn Mendes.

Chapter Seventeen

Terminating the Terminator

'I thought being President would be easier than my old life.'
- Donald Trump, 28 April 2017, Reuters Interview.

One of America's most popular television shows is *The Apprentice*, a reality program where contestants compete to become the 'Apprentice'. The contestant judged to have the highest business acumen wins the title, a large cash reward and a one year contract to run one of Donald Trump's companies.

The show is popular for two reasons. Firstly, people love to watch other people fail. Secondly, it showcases the American dream - that anyone can achieve anything if they work hard. This program effectively gives one average American the chance to become a powerful manager of an important company, even if that company could be a Trump toilet cleaning service in New Jersey.

Donald Trump was the host of this television show. He cleverly used the program to build up his own celebrity status, whilst also creating valuable relationships with celebrities via *The Celebrity Apprentice* spin-off. When Trump left the show to run for president, Arnold Schwarzenegger took over the role as host. The ratings were lower than when Trump hosted.

Schwarzenegger, a former actor and the former governor of California, is a vocal critic of Trump.

In June 2017, Schwarzenegger publicly came out against Trump, slamming his Muslim ban and referring to Trump's presidency as a hiccup for the country. His statement was:

> 'We do not have a dictatorship, we have a democracy and our Constitution has been written so well that it is bulletproof. We've gone through Watergate and all the different trouble, and America has always come out well. This is a little hiccup for America and it will work its way through it. You will see the reaction and the way it's all going to unravel...
>
> All I know is, when I see him going in the wrong direction, like he's done, we will go on the attack, we will go on social media and speak up. I mean that with no hostility. I don't believe everyone has to agree with everything I say.'

Readers will assume from the above that Schwarzenegger is an enemy of Trump's and part of the opposition. Despite having been a Republican governor, he is no supporter of the Republican President. This is correct, but it is not the complete story.

So what is the actual story surrounding Schwarzenegger's opposition to his Republican leader?

Born three months before Hillary Clinton on 30 July 1947 in Austria, Schwarzenegger would face a tough upbringing with strict parents. His father was Gustav Schwarzenegger, an Austrian who joined the Nazi Party voluntarily, before Austria was annexed by Germany. He served in the Austrian military from 1930 to 1937, before later becoming a police officer and joining the military police units. During World War II, he served in Poland, France, Belgium, Ukraine, Lithuania and Russia. He was not a particularly outstanding officer, being noted in his records as having average intellect, but was a calm and reliable person.

There are many who are disappointed that Schwarzenegger was born in Austria, as this would later prevent him from running for the presidency. However, given that his father was a Nazi (and voluntarily one, as opposed to being forced to join), it is highly unlikely that he ever would have been successful in securing nomination, even if he was born in America. This is because Nazis are not especially favoured, given their proclivities.

However, Schwarzenegger claims he did not have a good relationship with his father, who preferred his elder brother and doubted whether he was actually his biological son. This claim is greeted with some scepticism, as it is likely Schwarzenegger would want to distance himself as far as possible from his Nazi father in order to have a career in politics. Indeed, this link was widely explored during the 2003 California campaign when Schwarzenegger was governor.

From the age of fourteen he developed a strong passion for weights and began to participate in bodybuilding sports. He has stated that his father encouraged him into the sport.

When he left school, he joined the Austrian Army in 1965. This was mandatory in Austria at this time. He was not a loyal soldier and was jailed for one week in military prison, as he skipped training so he could attend a bodybuilding competition. His obsession with the sport was beginning to affect his other duties.

In 1966, he entered the Mr Universe competition and would take second place. Here is the first link Schwarzenegger has to Trump, who owned the Miss Universe competition. At a young age, both men were displaying their love of competitions that sexualise the human body.

Two years later, he would make the move to America, which he had apparently dreamed of since the age of ten. Schwarzenegger believed that his bodybuilding future would meet with greater success in the country. In 1970, he would take the title of Mr Olympia in a bodybuilding competition, and would then win it six further times.

On 13 December 1972 his father died from a stroke. Schwarzenegger did not attend the funeral. His reason? He first stated that he did not attend as he was training for a bodybuilding contest, although it is likely that the real reason was that he had developed a distant relationship and was not overly affected by his father's passing. Despite his subsequent flaws, Schwarzenegger was not a sympathiser of the Nazi Party and resented his father for having joined.

During the 1970s, he was a frequent steroid user (the drug being legal during this decade). He believed that the steroids were helpful to him in maintaining his muscle size and were vital in his competition success. Readers should note that the majority of bodybuilding contestants during this time were ardent-steroid users, as it was more commonly acceptable at this time.

Interestingly, a Dr Willi Heepe predicted that Schwarzenegger would face an early death due to a connection existing between steroid use and heart problems. Schwarzenegger then successfully sued the doctor for defamation, arguing that the man had no knowledge as to when he would die. Whilst some celebrities sue reporters for making false claims about their love life or drug use, Schwarzenegger sued a doctor for claiming he would die. This proves that Schwarzenegger has always been concerned with his mortality - a point that will become important later on in this chapter.

Whilst he was using steroids during the 1970s, he commenced his acting career. Knowing that he could not maintain a bodybuilding lifestyle that would pay the bills for ever, he wisely invested in his future by starring in movies such as *Stay Hungry* in 1976. His breakthrough film would not be until 1982 in the famous movie *Conan the Barbarian*, where he established himself as an action star.

In 1984, he would make his debut as the Terminator in the movie aptly named *The Terminator*. To this date, this is the role he is most known for. His other famous films include *Predator*, *Twins*, *Total Recall*, *Batman & Robin* and *The 6th Day*.

The 6th Day again comments on Schwarzenegger's obsession with his mortality, where humans are cloned in order to ensure that they live forever. Should a person die, they will simply be 're-born' by a new clone being created. However, this causes problems when a clone is made but the original is still alive...

During his acting career, Schwarzenegger was a registered Republican. This put him at odds with many of those in Hollywood who support the Democrats. In 2004, Schwarzenegger addressed the Republican National Convention and said:

> *'I finally arrived here in 1968. What a special day it was. I remember I arrived here with empty pockets but full of dreams, full of determination, full of desire. The presidential campaign was in full swing. I remember watching the Nixon-Humphrey presidential race on TV. A friend of mine who spoke German and English*

translated for me. I heard Humphrey saying things that sounded like socialism, which I had just left.

But then I heard Nixon speak. He was talking about free enterprise, getting the government off your back, lowering the taxes and strengthening the military. Listening to Nixon speak sounded more like a breath of fresh air. I said to my friend, I said, "What party is he?" My friend said, "He's a Republican." I said, "Then I am a Republican." And I have been a Republican ever since.'

Whilst some Republicans may attribute their party dedication to more tangible events, Schwarzenegger proudly claims that Richard Nixon converted him to the cause.

Throughout his acting career that commenced in the 1970s, Schwarzenegger would join many political causes, even assisting George H. W. Bush during a campaign rally. When asked in 1999 whether he would ever consider running for a political office himself, he responded by saying that he thought about it regularly. Clearly, the man was ambitious and wanted to secure a position.

On 6 August 2003, Schwarzenegger announced that he would run for Governor of California. He was the most well known candidate, although he had never previously held political office and his policy ideas were widely unknown. The whole nation watched the election with interest. After all, they had previously watched his efficiency as the Terminator and wanted to see if he could convert this to political office.

On 7 October 2003, only two months after he had nominated, he won the election. He believed that his mandate was to remove the gridlock from government. Deciding to intimidate his Democrat opponents, he labelled all Democrat state politicians as being 'girlie men.' He ignored the female Democrats.

Whilst originally viewed as a staunch Republican who detested the Democrat Party, he was keen to create a legacy within California. To do so, he knew that he needed to become more moderate or else many of his policies risked being repealed by a Democrat successor. He made the decision to appoint a Democrat as his Chief of Staff, which resulted in him becoming a more centralist Governor than before. In 2006, the mayor of San Francisco commented that Schwarzenegger was, 'becoming a Democrat… He's running back, not even to the centre. I would say centre-left.'

Schwarzenegger did not prove to be an overly effective governor. When he commenced his term, his approval ratings were as high as 89%. On his last day in office on 3 January 2011, his approval had dropped to 23%. Most controversially, before he left office Schwarzenegger, as is his Governor-power, reduced a sentence of Esteban Nunez, who had committed manslaughter, to half of what he was sentenced. This was greeted with outrage by the press, as Esteban was the son of one of Schwarzenegger's key political allies.

Once his tenure as Governor came to an end, many wondered what was next for the man. Would he retire? Would he return to acting? Or did he harbour deeper political ambitions? Did he aspire to taking the White House for himself, despite not having been born in America?

There can be no doubt that it is the latter. In 2013, he began to explore the possibility of running for president, being keen to run in the 2016 election. He was of the view (which would later be proven to be correct) that 2016 was the year for a Republican to win. The Democrats had eight years in the White House and the public was prepared to vote in another.

Schwarzenegger began to lobby Senators and Congressmen about changing the law that prevents him from taking the office. Of note, there are different theories in the law as to what would happen if a non-American born citizen won the election. Would the Supreme Court disqualify the candidate? Or would they view the winning candidate as having bypassed this requirement? Naturally, given how expensive it is to run a campaign for office, Schwarzenegger would want to be certain that a victory would actually give him the presidency and not a losing court case.

As he could not change the law, he decided that he would not run in the 2016 nomination for the Republican candidacy. He would bide his time instead, hoping that in the future his lobbying would prove successful. As a prominent Republican, he was asked during the campaign whether he endorsed Trump. He stated that he would not vote for Trump and this would be the first time he did not vote for the Republican candidate in the election. Schwarzenegger said:

> 'For the first time since I became a citizen in 1983, I will not vote for the Republican candidate for President.
>
> Like many Americans, I've been conflicted by this election - I still haven't made up my mind about how exactly I will vote next month. I have been a proud Republican since I moved to America in 1968 and I heard Nixon's words about getting the government off our backs, free trade, and defending our liberty with a strong military. That day I joined the party of Abraham Lincoln, Teddy Roosevelt, and Ronald Reagan.
>
> But as proud as I am to label myself a Republican, there is one label that I hold above all else - American. So I want to take a moment today to remind my fellow Republicans that it is not only acceptable to choose your country over your party - it is your duty.'

Naturally, this was after a different Republican (Mike Pence) had been selected as Trump's running mate.

As shown at the outset of this chapter, once Trump became President Trump, Schwarzenegger did not reduce his criticism. He has remained an opponent of the man. So what would lead this son of a Nazi, who converted to the Republicans because of Richard Nixon, to hate Trump so significantly? Was it simply a jealousy that existed between two celebrities? Or was there a different factor in play?

To put it bluntly, Schwarzenegger is a pawn of Shawn Mendes.

Shawn has previously invested in insurance policies, believing that Bernie Sanders could be a viable alternative if Trump failed. Once it became apparent to Shawn that this would not work, he began looking elsewhere for a new investment.

Schwarzenegger was the perfect man for Shawn to begin to manipulate. In late 2016, he contacted the man and they spoke about Schwarzenegger's future. It is noted that at this point, Schwarzenegger already resented Trump. He viewed him as an upstart and resented his popularity. He wanted the job for himself and he feared that Trump's victory would later turn the American public against non-Washington candidates. Whilst the American public would be prepared to experiment with a celebrity every now and then, they would not turn to them consistently.

By aligning himself with the bodybuilder, Shawn would be able to keep himself across the man's ambitions. Schwarzenegger was still lobbying Congress to change the law so he could run in 2020. He believed that the Republican nomination could become a celebrity battle, where the public would tune in as it would be like watching a celebrity reality show. This would generate free advertising and help in his push to take the White House.

The plan had some merit and Shawn was interested. Naturally, over time the public would begin to lose interest in Trump, as they did with every president. They would want a fresh approach. Perhaps the former Californian Governor was the future. Perhaps the bodybuilder could pull off the impossible and be the first elected non-American born President.

Shawn also had an ulterior motive in contacting Schwarzenegger. He wanted the law to be changed so that in the future he himself would be eligible to become President of the United States. As a Canadian born, he would be deemed just as ineligible as the Austrian.

Whilst some readers may believe this to be an incredibly risky ploy of Shawn, it is worth remembering that Schwarzenegger and Trump hate each other. They do not communicate and they do not share common allies. Whilst both noting themselves down as Republicans, their true loyalty is to their ambition. Neither would convey to the other that one of their advisers is Shawn Mendes, as this would not be in their own interests to do so.

Indeed, there are some sources who believe that Schwarzenegger only publicly criticises President Trump when Shawn is feeling aggrieved towards the White House. Comments from Schwarzenegger greatly irritate Trump, which leads him into a tirade on Twitter.

On 4 March 2017, Trump tweeted:

> *'Arnold Schwarzenegger isn't voluntarily leaving the Apprentice, he was fired by his bad (pathetic) ratings, not by me. Sad end to great show.'*

Schwarzenegger responded with the following press statement:

'Arnold is praying that President Trump can start improving his own approval ratings, which were the worst in history for an incoming president, by taking his job seriously and working inclusive-inclusively.'

Whilst Shawn may be working secretly with Schwarzenegger, it is not clear what his plans for the Terminator in the future entail. Would Shawn want to see Schwarzenegger elected to the White House? Or does he simply want to encourage the man to have the laws changed surrounding eligibility, and then dump him?

Shawn reportedly does not believe that Schwarzenegger will make a successful president, as shown by his history in California. Therefore, he may be of the view that he would not be the best person to take the title as a non-American born president. This would make it harder for future non-American born candidates (such as Shawn).

Just like with Bernie Sanders, it is highly likely that Shawn will use Schwarzenegger whilst it suits him, and then discard him once the man becomes a liability. In any event, by the next election Schwarzenegger will be 74 years old, which would make him the oldest President in history if he wins the election. With a plethora of younger, more popular candidates, Schwarzenegger's chances of securing the nomination are slim.

However, if Shawn were to change his mind and support the man, anything is possible.

Chapter Eighteen

Melania Trump Unleashed

'Can you imagine what the outcry would be if SnoopDogg, failing career and all, had aimed and fired the gun at President Obama? Jail time!'
- Donald Trump, 15 March 2017, Twitter.

'You came through for me and I am going to come through for you,' President Trump boomed out to the assembled members of the National Rifle Association (NRA).

The crowd roared their approval, ecstatic that for the first time in a decade they had a president in place supportive of their organisation's aims. They booed when images appeared of Hillary Clinton, hating the woman for daring to challenge their stance on weapons.

> *'The eight year assault on your Second Amendment freedoms has come to a crashing end. You now have a true friend and champion in the White House. I will never, ever infringe on the right of the people to keep and bear arms. Never ever.'*

His speech to the large crowd of NRA supporters marked the highpoint of his relationship with his group. During the election campaign, he relied heavily upon their support. At one point, he even suggested that if Hillary were to win the election, they could take action into their own hands:

> *'By the way, and if she gets to pick her judges, nothing you can do, folks. Although the Second Amendment people, maybe there is, I don't know.'*

The NRA backed Trump more heavily than any previous candidate. They spent three times more on his campaign than they did for Mitt Romney back in 2012. And Trump rewarded their support as soon as he was sworn in as President. In February 2017 he rolled back an Obama regulation that made it harder for people with diagnosed mental illnesses to purchase a gun. Essentially, there was no need for people to be restricted in buying a weapon if they were deemed unfit to handle their own financial affairs and had a mental illness.

Rejoice, the NRA screamed, for those that are now mentally unhinged can purchase weapons! This is the land of the free, after all.

The Moms Demand Action group was outraged, saying:

> *'NRA leaders are hoping their investment in the election will help them pass dangerous legislation that would enrich gun manufacturers while endangering Americans. This includes dismantling the criminal background check system, making gun silences more accessible, and - their ultimate goal - passing 'Concealed Carry Reciprocity'.'*

Trump's support for the NRA was unprecedented. Not only was he promising to not interfere with gun law, he was also pledging to rollback previous reforms that Obama had fought so hard for. What was Trump's strategy behind this? Was it that he himself was a strong advocate for guns, despite never having held one in his life? Had he suddenly developed a passion for weaponry and the military, despite avoiding the Vietnam War like the plague? Or was there a different factor involved?

To answer this question, we must first explore the NRA association itself.

Formed in 1871, the NRA is one of America's longest standing organisations. Further, it is also viewed as being in the top three most influential groups. Many congressmen and senators owe their election to financial support they have received from the NRA. These congressmen and senators then repay their debt by opposing any gun reform, securing the NRA's relevancy in America's society.

Whilst criticised by other nations, the NRA is relatively popular within American society. Over 82% of Republican voters are said to hold the group in a favourable light, whilst 55% of Democrats also support the group. Naturally, obtaining the support of the NRA during an election is vital.

Throughout political history, the NRA has had a number of key politicians as members of their group. For example, Theodore Roosevelt, William Howard Taft, Dwight D. Eisenhower, John F. Kennedy, Ronald Reagan, George H. W. Bush and Donald Trump were / are all NRA members. Further, two Chief Justices of the Supreme Court were also part of the NRA. This influence is remarkable.

However, they are currently headed by Melania Trump, the machine that Trump commissioned in Japan. Why would Melania head the NRA?

In 2014, the year before Trump would announce his candidacy for the Republican nomination, he programmed Melania to infiltrate the NRA. He wanted to ensure their support and secure a high level of funding for his campaign. To do so, he needed to have the NRA run by an ally. He was acutely aware that even Mitt Romney, a pro-NRA candidate, was unable to receive significant support from the group.

Melania, being a machine equipped with a high fighting ability, was able to use her powers to quickly rise up through the ranks of the NRA, whilst also not attracting the attention of the media. One NRA member told your correspondent:

> 'We all knew that she was coming in and out of headquarters all the time. We thought nothing of it. She was Donald's wife and he was a keen supporter of our group, so it made sense that she would attend all of our functions on his behalf. Plus, she was easy on the eyes so no one complained that she was always coming in. Peter Brownell, who is currently our official president, was always having meetings with her.
>
> In 2014, a secret vote was held by the exclusive members, of which I am one. Melania nominated to be our leader, but said that due to her husband's public profile she could not be revealed as the new president. That could hurt him in the polls and raise questions over conflicts of interest. We all understood this. We don't really like the government and the press meddling in the affairs of private citizens, so everyone agreed that if she did win, she would not be

135

named as president but rather a proxy would be appointed in her place. She would then just control everything from behind closed doors. Obviously she won and that is what occurred…

How did she win? Well, to be honest, most of her opponents went mysteriously missing the day before the vote. We haven't heard from them since. She was the only candidate running so it was a pretty easy win. All credit to her.'

There are also unconfirmed reports that Melania's acceptance speech was copied word for word from Michelle Obama.

Melania would prove to be one of the most effective leaders the NRA ever had. Her history of being a security guard to Trump would serve her well in advocating on gun-related issues, as she understood the importance of having weaponry to defend people.

The source also told your correspondent:

'When Trump announced in 2015, there was plenty of talk about whether we should support Donald or not. Some in the group thought he was too unpredictable for us to spend our funds on, and instead we should invest in supporting new Senators as that would be a longer investment. Presidents can only serve a maximum of eight years, so once that is done, the investment is done. Senators and congressmen can be in there forever, so that way we get a bigger return for our buck.

Melania was really passionate that we should direct all of our support to Donald and slam Hillary as much as possible. She kept repeating the same line that Hillary would cut off our access to guns and Donald was the only one that could save us. Some members freaked out and said that we had to support him straight away. Others said that Melania was exaggerating for her own purposes.

Funnily enough, all those members who opposed the idea went missing. I still don't know where they are.'

Shawn Mendes staunchly opposed the plan to place Melania as the head of the NRA. He argued that it was her primary role to serve as Trump's security guard and that her appointment with the NRA would distract her from her duties. His criticism was ignored by Trump, who wanted the NRA to support him.

Machines and artificial intelligence are continuing to grow in today's society, with many being concerned that eventually AI will go too far and that humans may be placed at risk by our machine counterparts. Melania, whilst only imprinted with a small amount of AI, began to develop during the campaign. She realised that Shawn opposed her as the head of the NRA. Accordingly, in 2016 she told CNN that as First Lady her aim was to combat cyber bullying and cited social media (Shawn's domain) as being a beacon of bullying.

Given that few people listen when the machine Melania speaks, it is highly unlikely that Shawn interpreted this comment as a slight against him.

So what next for the NRA? This is the first time in their history that they have the First Lady (and a machine to boot) as the head of their organisation. This provides them with an unparalleled level of influence and a direct link to the White House.

But who is really influencing who? Is the NRA influencing Trump through Melania? Or is Melania influencing the NRA for Trump? Accounts differ on this point. The NRA is always going to support the Republican Party during presidential elections. Republicans, after all, are more pro-gun than their Democrat counterparts. It would be foolish for a pro-gun organisation to back a candidate likely to propose measures that are against their best interests.

This meant that the NRA was always going to inject funds into Trump's campaign, but the extent of this was unclear. Having only supported Romney in a lukewarm matter, it made sense that Trump wanted to infiltrate the group to boost this support and harm Hillary. But Trump is more publicly pro weaponry than Mitt Romney was. There is a school of thought that Trump would always have secured more funding from the group than Romney. Here was an electable candidate proposing to give the NRA everything they wanted and all they needed to do was support him. Why would they not throw their considerable weight behind him?

And why did Trump go against Shawn's advice during such a critical juncture? Trump effectively placed his own life at risk by diverting Melania to head the NRA. Every time that she visited the NRA, she was not by his side, ready to use her body as a shield to ward off an angry voter who, ironically, would use a weapon against him. Was the extra few million dollars really worth losing such a valuable security guard?

Readers are reminded about Ivanka Trump's witch skills and the level of influence she has over her father. Ivanka is not Melania's daughter and it is reported that there is a certain level of tension between the machine and the human.

It is highly possible that Ivanka wanted to remove Melania as much as possible. By influencing her father through witchcraft to send the robot to the NRA, she would get rid of the machine for some time. Further, it would allow her in the future to use Melania in other organisations, rendering her father defenceless.

And why would Ivanka want Trump to lose his most trusted security guard? Was Ivanka herself plotting? Or was it purely out of womanly/robotly jealousy?

A White House source told your correspondent:

> 'I have seen them eating dinner together. It is always very cold between them. They share a cold smile, but nothing more. There is no conversation. No warmth. I think Ivanka laughed once, but that was after Melania was accused of ripping off Michelle's speech. Ivanka thought that was hilarious. President Trump was not pleased at all with the growing divide between the two women, telling them both that they needed to act like grown-ups and work together, as the only woman he wanted to oppose was Hillary, who he blamed for causing the tension between them. Although to be fair, he does blame Hillary for a lot. When his coffee is too cold. When the shower is too hot. When he does not get his glass of milk at the right time. It is all Hillary's fault.'

Chapter Nineteen

The Con's Way

'Any negative polls are fake news, just like the CNN, ABC, NBC polls in the election. Sorry, people want border security and extreme vetting.'
- Donald Trump, 6 February 2017, Twitter.

It takes a special kind of political deviant to switch from candidate to candidate, without carrying any baggage. Most politicians will not trust the former staff or advisers of their adversaries, suspecting that they may have an ulterior motive.

Shawn Mendes was able to flit from the Hillary camp to the Trump camp solely because Trump wanted him on his side. His involvement with Bernie Sanders and Arnold Schwarzenegger only was successful because neither man realised Shawn's involvement with their opponents. Had they known, it is likely he would have been shown the door.

Yet Kellyanne Conway is an interesting figure. She served as Trump's campaign manager during the election (having been the only woman to ever run a successful presidential campaign) and now has the title 'Counselor to the President'. Before she did this, she endorsed Ted Cruz for the candidacy and served on his political action committee. Once Cruz withdrew from the race on Shawn's command, Trump decided to approach Conway with a job offer.

Since working for Trump, she has become a notorious figure, known for creating the term 'alternative facts', making up massacres and endorsing commercial products in her government position.

So how did Kellyanne Conway secure the support of Trump, despite having worked for his opponent? Was she included in the murder of Cruz and his replacement as a robot? Is she a robot herself, just like Melania Trump?

To date, the Trump Administration has failed to answer any of these questions. Even more suspiciously, these questions have never been asked. Clearly, somebody is hiding something.

Born on 20 January 1967 in New Jersey, Conway would spend her childhood being raised by powerful women. After her parents divorced when she was three, she was raised by her mother, grandmother and two aunts.

When she finished high school she went on to study a Bachelor of Arts at Trinity College in Washington D.C. Following this, she received a Juris Doctor from the George Washington University Law School and would go on to serve as a judicial clerk for a Superior Court judge in Columbia.

She considered joining a law firm, but found that her passion was in polling. She obtained a job with Luntz Research Companies, specialising in polling services. In 1995 she started her own business, the Polling Company, that served Republican politicians. Some of her key clients included the Speaker of the House, Newt Gingrich, and the then Congressman Mike Pence. In 2012, Gingrich hired her to act as his senior adviser, a role which she cherished. However, Gingrich was not successful in obtaining the nomination.

Her position as a pollster attracted the interest of media companies who would have her appear as a political commentator. She has appeared on ABC, CBS, PBS, CNN and the Fox News Channel, amongst others.

Before the 2016 election, she had already established herself as a strong political figure with the potential to be an asset to any team. She was obsessed with numbers and enjoyed manipulating polls to her own advantage.

As a Republican pollster, many candidates were keen to get her endorsement and have her join their team. Both the Trump camp and the Cruz camp approached her with job offers. Shawn Mendes himself was particularly enthusiastic about engaging Conway, as he believed she could be used to supplement his social media skills by providing raw data that they could then target Facebook direct advertisements with.

Conway decided that Ted Cruz was the more electable of the two and publicly endorsed him before joining his political action committee. She then publicly slammed Trump, calling him 'extreme' and 'not a conservative'. On 25 January 2016 she stated, 'Trump is a man who seems to be offending his way to the nomination. Donald Trump has literally bulldozed over the little guy to get his way.'

However, over time Conway realised she was not impressed with Cruz. He seemed too robotic for her liking (to this date, Conway still does not realise that Trump had Cruz murdered and replaced with a machine). Once Cruz pulled out of the race, Trump again approached Conway with the encouragement of Shawn.

Given that Trump does not forgive those who insult him, some readers may question why Trump would try to solicit her support once more. After all, her criticism of him was blunt and it was clear she had no respect for him. What he did have respect for, however, was her blind ambition and her knowledge of polling numbers. Trump needed somebody on his team with the knack of pinpointing the exact locations he needed to target to ensure that he would win the election. There was no one better in the country than Conway for this job. Pushing aside past differences, he decided (for once) to swallow his ego and engage her.

Naturally, Conway accepted the offer. She was ambitious and wanted to join the presidential campaign. Besides, the cheque on offer was substantial.

On 1 July 2016 Trump gladly announced that Conway was hired to be his senior adviser. One month later, she was promoted to be his campaign manager, after the previous two had been fired. She would prove to be an effective weapon for the Trump team, leading the campaign in the last ten weeks and driving in the advantage he held over Hillary. She was a merciless woman and would go on the attack when needed and drilled her offence-ethos into Trump. Nothing was off limits, as far as she was concerned. Her theme was 'win at any cost.'

Once Trump won the election, he offered Conway a White House job. Conway, in a show of confidence in her own ability, tweeted, 'I can have any job I want.' This boast was met with disdain by some, but Trump, a serial Tweeter, appreciated the honesty of her post.

When Trump was considering appointing Mitt Romney as his Secretary of State, Conway tweeted, 'Receiving deluge of social media & private comms re: Romney. Some Trump loyalists warn against Romney as sec of state.'

Trump was not pleased with this tweet. He believed that the discussions he had with her regarding cabinet appointments should be kept private and he told her that under no circumstances was she to tweet private and confidential information about the White House which could threaten the nation's security - that was his job to do. It was then reported by the CNBC that Trump was becoming frustrated at her failure to become a team player and viewed her as a divisive figure within the administration.

Originally, Conway wanted to become the Secretary of Education. However, due to Trump slowly losing confidence in her ability to maintain a cool head, he decided to appoint her as his formal adviser instead. She would also act as a spokeswoman for the administration, making regular media appearances to defend Trump's policies.

Her media appearances would be met with much ridicule by the press, who began to view the woman as a bumbling idiot, the perfect example of the Trump administration. Supporters viewed her as an efficient mouthpiece not ashamed to speak her mind.

Her first controversial appearance was when she defended Sean Spicer claiming falsities on Trump's inauguration. Conway stated that he was simply using alternative facts, which reminded everybody of the dystopian novel *1984* by George Orwell, where the government uses 'double-speak' to trick the public into believing falsehoods. After she said this, sales of *1984* increased by 9,500% and made the book the number one bestseller on Amazon. Naturally, Amazon was thrilled by her terminology.

On 2 February 2017 she appeared on television to defend Trump's controversial immigration ban, by referring to an event caused by Iraqi terrorists and labelled the 'Bowling Green Massacre'. The only issue with her defence of the policy was that this massacre had never occurred. Nobody knew what she was referring to.

On 9 February 2017, she was then criticised for violating ethical laws surrounding her position in a government role. She criticised Nordstrom's decision to drop products supplied by Ivanka's company, saying, 'Go buy Ivanka's stuff is what I would tell you. It's a wonderful line. I own some of it. I'm going to give a free commercial here: Go buy it today, everybody. You can find it online.'

This was a controversial move. Whilst Conway's supporters claimed she was not using her position to endorse or advertise Ivanka's products, the issue was that Conway herself said 'I'm going to give a free commercial here'. There was no denying that she had publicly endorsed a commercial product closely tied to the White House.

Sean Spicer, an ally of Conway, came out to say, 'Kellyanne has been counselled, and that's all we are going to go with... She's been counselled on the subject, and that's it.'

Then, on 15 February 2017 the television program *Morning Joe* announced she would be banned from appearing on the show. This was a startling position, as Conway was a member of the Trump administration. The co-host of the program said, 'We know for a fact that she tries to book herself on this show. I won't do it. Because I don't believe in fake news, or information that is not true... every time I've ever seen her on television, something's askew, off or incorrect.'

The program was effectively saying that she was an unreliable source and they did not want to spread her fake news on television.

On 13 February 2017, her fallout with key ally Sean Spicer commenced. Conway publicly claimed that Michael Flynn, the then National Security Adviser, had Trump's full confidence and there was no truth to the rumours that a gulf existed between them. Within three hours, Flynn resigned and left the White House.

Conway then claimed the next day that he offered to resign, despite Spicer claiming the complete opposite - that Trump had asked for his resignation.

She was furious at this inconsistency existing between their stories. It was one thing to try to trick the public, it was another to try to trick the public with two alternative facts. They simply would not believe this. Conway decided that Spicer had to go, as they were not on the same level. She began to leak stories to the press that Trump was agitated with Spicer. This led to Spicer's eventual dismissal.

Despite all of the above, there have been rumours suggesting Conway detests her job and does not agree with the policies of Trump. If this is true, why did she accept a job as his adviser? Why has she remained at the White House?

As previously stated, Conway is ambitious. Whilst before the 2016 election she was known in Republican circles, she was not widely known by the public. Obsessed with gaining media spots to defend Trump, she is doing her best to have her face and name out in the public eye to boost brand recognition. Basically, Conway is yet another person hoping to contest the 2020 election.

Given that she is a powerful pollster with strong connections and a public image, she would make for an interesting candidate. Is the Republican Party ready for a female candidate? Could Conway secure the same support Trump did? Would she be able to compete against Trump in 2020?

No. For the people that are assuming Conway is planning to run for president in the 2020 election, they are completely wrong. She has no intentions of doing so, knowing that now is not her time. Rather, she wishes to compete as the running mate for another candidate in 2020 - Shawn Mendes.

Astute readers will remember that Shawn was the one who encouraged Trump to engage with Conway, in order to utilise her powerful polling methods. But Shawn knows that Conway held back on some of her abilities during the election, not wanting to reveal all of her secrets to the Republican Party's war machine, or else they would not need her in the future.

With her skills of being able to utilise polls to identify weak points in a campaign and manipulate figures to result in boosts, she would make a key ally to any presidential hopeful. Statistics and maths can win an election, if combined with charisma. Shawn would bring that, and his fame, to their push for office in 2020.

This is why Conway is prepared to embarrass herself regularly on television. She knows, after closely observing the Bernie Sanders campaign, that it is better to be talked about negatively than not at all.

Sanders was not criticised by the press. He was simply ignored. And as a result, his poll numbers declined considerably.

Trump faced the opposite situation. He was criticised constantly by the press, but he was still in the media. This boosted his polling figures. Should the public not hear from a candidate at all, they will begin to assume that person is weak and does not have any policy ideas. Eventually, negative criticism will fall into white noise and the public will stop listening.

Conway is more than happy to accept criticism. She understands that over time the public will begin to tune out when people mock her, as they will be sick of hearing the same thing over and over again. This will make her immune to negativity, whilst keeping her name and image in the public's eye. By the time 2020 is here, she will be a readymade Vice President.

Even better for Conway, there is a high likelihood that in the future she will be fired by Trump, who likes to occasionally fire his staff to keep the rest motivated. Given Trump's declining popularity, this will serve to bolster her own stocks and she can use this as a point of difference in the 2020 nomination. Conway, being a pollster, is not necessarily a member of the establishment and can still attract the anti-establishment votes.

But does Shawn want Conway as a running mate, if he even is planning to run in 2020? Would he not be better suited to take on Schwarzenegger? This is not clear, as Shawn is attempting to maintain a public image (at least for those in the know) that he and Trump are still on civil terms. By aligning himself with Conway, he would be declaring war.

Shawn is a strong believer in insurance policies and is happy to humour political stars who want his support. This way he does not place all of his eggs in one basket and has a variety of options to select from, should the time come that he is no longer allied to Trump.

Conway herself would have no reason to doubt that Shawn would want her assistance. After all, he leant heavily on her during the 2016 election and was keen to engage her services. She was humbled by his interest and was in awe of the close relationship he had with Trump. She is one of the few people in the world who knew that Shawn acted as an adviser to Trump, because Shawn believed she was trustworthy enough to keep this secret.

On her ambitions, a White House source told your correspondent that:

> *'President Trump knows she is hungry for his job. That's why he hired her in the first place. He wants the drive to motivate her to do everything possible to please him. He hates being surrounded by idiots.*
>
> *There's also another funny reason President Trump is happy for her to be there. She and his daughter Ivanka do not get on well at all. They hate each other. Both want to take the job. President Trump wants them to motivate each other, so that one day they can be rivals. He thinks having a good rival is an ingredient for success.'*

If it is true that Trump believes Ivanka and Conway hate each other, it would produce ample reason for the two to compete in the 2020 nomination. However, Ivanka would only compete if Trump was no longer planning on running, or she influenced him using her witchery to not run.

There would then be a race between two very powerful women (along with any others who may decide to throw their hat in the ring).

Is Shawn then simply using Conway as a balance to Ivanka? Is he fearful of her use of witchcraft and believes that she will truly be a threat one day?

Possibly. This rivalry is in the best interests of Shawn, as it prevents Ivanka from aligning herself with Conway. If these two ever were to team up, it would be a dangerous combination.

Some readers may believe that Conway did ally herself with Ivanka when she endorsed her products. After all, if Conway hated Ivanka, why would she tell the public to go out and buy her product? This is because Conway knew that she herself was not popular at the time. Any endorsement from Conway is effectively a kiss of death. No one will go and buy a product because a woman, who is well known for sprouting alternative facts, said the product was good quality. People would instead assume that the product was faulty and buy a competing product instead.

This is exactly what happened. Ivanka suspects that Conway did it on purpose to harm her own commercial ventures and reduce her wealth so she had less funds to launch her future presidential campaign.

Conway outplayed Ivanka in this scenario, showing that she is an astute political operator and will pose a danger to anyone opposing her in 2020. By all accounts, Conway will be contesting in 2020, regardless of whether Shawn nominates her as his running mate or not. She is ambitious, and she has gone the con-way with the public for far too long to back out.

Chapter Twenty

Dwayne Johnson

'Watched protests yesterday but was under the impression that we just had an election! Why didn't these people vote? Celebs hurt cause badly.'
- Donald Trump, 22 January 2017, Twitter.

By now, readers will recognise that there has been a common theme in American politics since President Trump secured victory in 2016 - there are many people considering contending for the throne in 2020.

On the Democrat side, Michelle Obama is already being touted as a future candidate. She impressed during her tenure as First Lady and delivered powerful speeches against Trump in 2016. Indeed, her slogan 'When they go low, we go high' has been quoted by many as being an example of being dignified in opposition. Whilst other candidates are yet to come to the forefront, readers can be rest assured that the Democrat Party is filled with ambitious individuals wanting to vie for the crown.

On the Republican side, Arnold Schwarzenegger is considering running in 2020, provided his lobbying to have the law changed is successful. Ivanka Trump, President Trump's daughter, will also run provided she has her father's voluntary/involuntary blessing. Kellyanne Conway is eager to run as Vice President.

Some political pundits believe Ted Cruz may run, as it is publicly believed few dislike Trump more than the Senator. After all, he had to suffer through Trump criticising how his wife looks and the suggestion that his father may have been involved in the assassination of John F.

Kennedy. However, as he is a robot controlled by Trump, it is unlikely he will ever pose a serious threat to the Trump administration.

Senator Jeff Flake from Arizona is viewed as a contender able to appeal to the centre of the Republican Party. He has written a book highly critical of Trump and believes that the Republican Party should not support him. Admired by politicians on both sides, he is viewed as a man who could potentially heal the divide. However, Trump, as previously stated does not like criticism nor forget it, has already approached several candidates to contest Flake's seat before the 2020 election, and thus make him vulnerable.

Then there is Governor John Kasich from Ohio, who was the most influential Republican that refused to endorse Trump during the 2016 election. He has been asked whether he would run in 2020 and replied with:

> '*I'm going to finish my term in 18 months as governor of our state, pull the state together and get it to do better and better and better. That's what I'm all about - and giving everybody a shot. And then I don't know what I'm going to do. I'm going to keep a voice, but I can't predict to you - I never thought I would be governor, I never thought I'd go back into politics.*'

Governor Scott Walker of Wisconsin ran in the 2016 bid but failed quickly. Many people do not even recall that he did nominate, such was his short-lived campaign. His low profile is viewed as a plus. Some believe Republican voters will be eager for a leader who does not make the news every five minutes, nor put the country in peril by a midnight tweet.

Lastly, Senator Ben Sasse is viewed as an up and coming leader, not just because his last name makes him sound sassy. As a senator from Nebraska, he has not been backward in coming forward in his criticism of Trump, being happy to represent himself as an alternative to the loud leader.

With such a large field of potential candidates, there is no guarantee that Trump will nominate, or win, the 2020 nomination for the Republican Party. Many within the Republican Party regret their choice of endorsing Trump, believing him to be a divisive leader that will have long-term negative impacts on their party.

So who is most likely to challenge Donald Trump for the 2020 Republican nomination? Who poses the greatest threat to the billionaire real estate mogul?

Surprisingly, it is not one of the people mentioned above. Despite these candidates being widely touted, none is expected to bring the clout required to defeat Trump. But for critics of Trump, fear not, for there is a candidate with a large profile planning on a 2020 push. He has even gone on the record to say that he is considering this.

Who is this mysterious man?

Dwayne Johnson. Or more commonly known as 'The Rock'.

Born on 2 May 1972 to a wrestling family, he would grow up listening to stories from his father about his wrestling days. From a very young age, the passion of wrestling would be instilled into The Rock.

He was born in California and has Samoan blood in him. During his childhood, he spent a brief time in New Zealand before returning to the United States and then attending high school in Hawaii. Because he played football incredibly well, he was offered a full scholarship to the University of Miami and studied a Bachelor of General Studies, majoring in criminology and physiology.

In 1995, The Rock told his father that he was interested in wrestling and wanted to be trained. His father was reluctant at first, knowing full well how vigorous the training was and that it would change his life forever. Eventually though, he agreed and training was commenced. The following year, The Rock made his debut in the WWF. There was significant media attention surrounding his debut, as he was WWF's first third generation wrestler.

For those readers who are not familiar with WWF, which stands for World Wrestling Federation (now called WWE, World Wrestling Entertainment), it is a wrestling competition that is completely fake. The major events of the fight are prepared beforehand and the outcome is decided, even before the wrestlers come into the stadium.

The Rock received the favour of WWF during his time. As his father and grandfather had worked for the organisation, they pushed his presence, despite his character of The Rock originally being unpopular and receiving many jeers from the crowds.

He would continue to 'compete' in the WWF until 2004.

At this point, and in the interests of full disclosure, your correspondent should reveal that he once played as The Rock on WWF on Nintendo 64. Because the character lost the match, your correspondent has been bitter towards The Rock ever since. However, your correspondent is mature and will not let this bitterness get in the way of objective reporting.

Whilst The Rock, who is a despicable person, competed in wrestling, he also commenced his acting career. In 1999, he made his debut by starring in an episode of *That '70s Show*. A year later, he made an appearance in *Star Trek: Voyager*.

The Rock then turned to Hollywood and featured in his first movie in 2001 with *The Mummy Returns*. In 2002 he starred in *The Scorpion King*; in 2003 he was in *The Rundown*; in 2004 *Walking Tall*. Other movies that he has starred in include *Doom, Get Smart, The Game Plan* and *Southland Tales*.

Not being content with acting alone, The Rock also invested in starting his own production company, that has produced several films including *Baywatch* and *Jumanji: Welcome to the Jungle*.

His long career notwithstanding, his greatest achievement occurred in 2015 when he achieved the world record for taking the most selfies in three minutes. An enviable achievement.

Despite all of the above successes, The Rock went bankrupt in 2016, before once again building up his wealth with his television show *Ballers*.

So how has any of this led to a potential political career?

The Rock has previously been active in politics. In 2000, he attended the Democrat National Convention as part of a campaign to get more young people to vote. He was a supporter of the Republican Party that year and also attended the Republican National Convention. As of 2017, he had listed himself as an independent.

In 2017, The Rock visited the television show *Saturday Night Live* and jokingly stated that he would run for President, with Tom Hanks as his running mate. However, in July 2017 paperwork was officially filed with the Federal Electoral Commission for The Rock to run for President in 2020. When the *Washington Post* published an article that opined The Rock could win the 2020 election, The Rock went onto Instagram to respond:

> *'Interesting piece from The Washington Post on if I ran for POTUS I could actually win. Writer Alyssa Rosenberg did some pretty good research into my background (slave descendants fighting for their freedom, Revolutionary War etc). Much more to uncover but well done.*
>
> *More and more pieces like this are popping up due to the Presidential election and they're cool/fun to read… I care DEEPLY about our country… and the idea of one day becoming President to create real positive impact and global change is very alluring.*
>
> *Buuuuut until that possible day, the most important thing right now is strong honest leadership from our current and future leaders of this country. Thanks again Washington Post.'*

Whilst The Rock later deleted the above post, it was clear that he had already begun speaking like a politician. Not only did he express his love for America, but he also managed to take credit for historical slave uprisings. It seemed that The Rock would be a natural candidate.

But could he become President of the United States? Surely a man who has never had a real job in his life, has flirted with bankruptcy laws and only has experience being a television personality could never legitimately run for the White House? President Trump said that the entire idea was ridiculous and the American public would see past such a hare-brained scheme.

The Rock seems to think he has the skill set to make a real difference to American politics. And perhaps he does. There is no hard and fast rule that only a politician can run for the White House, as Trump has shown and Ronald Reagan before him.

But which party would The Rock nominate for? Would he go back to his old Republican Party? Would he flirt with the idea of becoming a Democrat? Or would he run as an independent, given he is currently calling himself one?

Readers should note that Bernie Sanders called himself an independent, right up until he decided to nominate for the Democrat candidacy.

The Rock himself has admitted to being seriously interested in the role, even telling Jimmy Fallon that he would be a relatable President the country needs. American voters from across the country could easily relate to the millionaire wrestler turned actor, as he is just like them.

A poll, that was not run by Conway's company, put Johnson at 42% support amongst the public compared to 37% for Trump. Based on this alone, he would defeat Trump in any contest. However, the next election is not until 2020 which is awhile away. Anything can occur between now and then.

Yet if this were the case, why has Trump not tweeted about The Rock? Whenever the President perceives a threat, he fires off a quick tweet to criticise the person, believing that his tweets have great power.

In an explosive revelation, your correspondent can now reveal that Trump is planning on The Rock to be his running mate in 2020, after he abandons Mike Pence for an upgraded version who is not gluten intolerant.

Trump loves celebrities. He enjoys surrounding himself with them. This is why he had Melania created as a beautiful robot and hired Shawn Mendes as his adviser. He wants people to know that he knows all of the right people. To have a celebrity as his Vice President would be his dream. People may know Mike Pence, but for the wrong reasons. Pence never defeated people in the wrestling ring. Pence never starred in a Hollywood blockbuster. Pence is boring. The Rock is fun and new. Not to mention, this provides Trump with funny material that he can tweet about.

Yet his advisers are not overly keen on this idea. Conway is against it because she has advised that Trump needs someone who has a powerful support base in a swinging state which her polling identifies is at risk. Trump should select the governor from that state, if they are Republican, or an influential senator. Shawn is against it because he wants Pence to remain, given that he is blackmailing the man into submission. Plus, he is wary The Rock may make Trump too popular, which would make it less easy to influence the man. And Ivanka Trump is against the idea because if her father does not agree to let her run in 2020, she wants to be his running mate. He has previously promised her just as much.

But Trump is the President. He believes he won the White House on his own. As the days go by, he is less and less likely to listen to the advice of his advisers, preferring to trust his own gut instinct. And his gut is telling him one thing - that he needs The Rock by his side.

This added celebrity status will help his campaign even more. He salivates at the idea of the free press coverage he would receive as a result. How will the Democrats compete against The Rock? If Michelle Obama dares to contest the election, The Rock can simply pick her up and throw her. Simple.

But The Rock has expressed no desire to be Trump's deputy. He has even gone on the public record, albeit very softly, to criticise the man. The Rock wants the President to be more inclusive and more 'relatable', which only he believes he can do. Trump is far too wealthy to ever be a man of the people. The Rock, having served time for his country as a wrestler, could be exactly what America needs.

Even though he wants the top job, The Rock may be tempted by Trump's offer. He has no previous political experience and a term as Vice President would show the American people that he is capable of running the country. But this could taint him with the Trump administration and make it harder to secure the nomination. Further, he would have to compete against Ivanka Trump, who does not want any more rivals.

And then there is another person, who has not yet been spoken about in this book for he only plays a very small role, Donald Trump Junior, Trump's first son.

With the honour of being named after a great man, Trump Junior cuts a classy figure in Washington circles. He most recently tweeted on Halloween he was going to take half of his daughter's candy away and tell her he gave it to another child who sat at home and did not trick or treat. This was to teach her about socialism.

Aside from sharing the same name, Trump Junior shares many characteristics with his father. He married a model and is a former realty television star.

Surprisingly, and impressively, Trump Junior is less popular than his father. In 2020 he was photographed after he hunted down an endangered leopard and after cutting off an elephant's tail. Trump

Junior is not as politically aware as his father - he was surprised when the public was outraged that he mutilated an elephant.

Trump Junior is also just as controversial as his father on Twitter. During the election, he posted an image of Skittles and asked his followers, 'If I had a bowl of skittles and I told you just three would kill you. Would you take a handful? That's our Syrian refugee problem'. Skittles were not impressed that he used their delicious product to make a point about the Syrian civil war.

Later on in the campaign, Trump Junior would compare the media's approach to airing stories about Hillary Clinton to that used by Nazi Germany during the Holocaust. This was also received poorly by the public.

Despite being voted less popular than stale McDonald's chips and the economy, Trump Junior believes he should be his father's running mate and successor in the 2020 election. Trump Junior has told his father that as he is the eldest child, he should be preferred to Ivanka.

President Trump, however, has different plans for his son. He believes that the best position for Trump Junior is to serve as Ambassador to the Russian Federation, given his Russian links and connections. Whenever the President opens the morning newspaper, all he sees are articles on how closely connected his son is with Russia. This, to Trump, proves that his son is the best man for the job.

Trump Junior is reportedly furious that Ivanka is being considered before him. If he were also to discover that his father is considering The Rock, a man who is highly unlikely to be the President's son, as Vice President, Trump Junior may decide to take action into his own hands and compete against his father in the 2020 election.

This would make for a very interesting battle. How would Republican voters decide on who to vote for - Donald Trump or Donald Trump? Would the Republican voters become confused and end up voting for the wrong Trump, which would divide the Trump vote and lead a third party to win the vote?

If Trump Junior does decide to elect, this will throw a spanner in the works for Trump's 2020 plans. His best course of action is to somehow placate his son before 2020, to prevent him from nominating. It is clear that the Russian appointment will not work and a more powerful position is required. If the Vice Presidency is not available, would the Secretary of State role suffice?

President Trump himself would be thrilled if his son accepted this job. As the President has said in his own words, 'The more Donald Trumps we have in power, the better. I envisage a world where Donald Trump holds every position known to man.'

Chapter Twenty One

The Fallout

*'My Twitter has become so powerful
that I can actually make my enemies tell the truth.'*
- Donald Trump, 17 October 2012, Twitter.

In 2016, Donald Trump achieved what many said he could not do. He won the election for the Presidency of the United States of America. In 2017, he was sworn in as President.

Since then, President Trump has proved to be a controversial figure, implementing an immigration ban, branding all Muslims as terrorists and wanting to build a wall to keep the Mexicans out (or one Mexican in particular).

But he has not achieved this alone. After snatching Shawn Mendes from the Hillary Clinton camp, Trump has used the pop sensation as his most trusted adviser. Behind every key decision, Shawn was there, whispering in his ear.

At the start, Shawn was young and Trump believed that he could manipulate the singer into only working for him. But over time Shawn has become ambitious and has begun to plot his own future, sometimes to the detriment of Trump.

From 2015 to the start of 2017, both Donald Trump and Shawn Mendes worked in harmony. Together, they used the robotic Ted Cruz after having the Senator murdered. They accidentally killed off David Bowie. They placed Carrie Fisher under arrest and had her frozen. They plotted to keep James Corden out of the United States by

building a wall along the Mexican border. And they maintained close ties with Russia.

Shawn's social media experience greatly helped the Trump campaign dominate this area. By creating fake news and using Russia to purchase Facebook advertisements, many Americans were left with negative views of Hillary Clinton.

Hillary did herself no favours during the campaign. Whilst she tried to outwit the Trump / Shawn duo by using the FBI Director to her own advantage, Comey could not be easily played. Or rather, he could not be played for long and skirted between the two camps regularly, which resulted in Hillary losing her election winning support.

Hillary knew about Trump hiring Shawn, but did nothing to reveal it to the public. She would not gain anything by disclosing this information, as she herself had used Shawn's services. It would only result in both her and Trump being discredited, with no clear winner.

As the campaign progressed, Shawn began to explore alternatives to Trump, in the event that his man did not win the presidency. He supported Bernie Sanders, encouraging him to leave his status as an independent and join the Democrats. He then abandoned Sanders, realising that Trump would turn on him if he did not win.

Shawn also opposed Trump's plan to place Melania as head of the NRA, believing that she was more suited to her security role. Trump went with advice from his daughter, Ivanka, over Shawn, and the divide between the two men started to grow.

After winning the presidency, Trump's decision to sack Sean Spicer was at odds with advice from Shawn. Again, the two continued to grow apart.

It is strongly believed by White House sources that the relationship has hit a point of no return, and Trump now rarely requests Shawn's opinion on matters:

'President Trump started to believe that he alone knew what was right. He was going to make a decision and then everybody else should enforce it. No question.

This led to him becoming quite distant with people that he previously relied on. He started to become lukewarm towards Conway, believing that she was getting too high of an opinion of herself. He

sacked Spicer. He no longer trusted Republilcan Governors that had
endorsed him, thinking that they themselves were going to run in
2020 against him. His paranoia has started to spin out of control.'

Shawn is reportedly quite aghast at the decline in his relationship with President Trump, believing that he has only ever provided the best advice to the man.

So where to next for the pop sensation? Will he attempt to rebuild the relationship with the President, hoping to gain his influence back? Or will he seek out another, who he can more easily manipulate?

Some readers by now may believe that Shawn Mendes is an ardent supporter of the Republican Party and is destined to follow in the plan foreshadowed by Kellyanne Conway. That is, he is to run for President in 2020, after the Terminator successfully lobbies Congress to have the law changed, and Conway is to become Vice President.

If this were to happen, he would likely face opposition in a Trump / The Rock running team. But which Trump that will be, is still questionable. Trump may be content with only serving one term. The President does not like to lose. His business strategy is all about winning. If he anticipates that he would not win the 2020 election, he will not contest it. He may even resign before 2020 so he leaves of his own accord, rather than what is dictated by others. If he does do this, Ivanka Trump will end up running for the 2020 candidacy, with her father's full support. Trump will no doubt suggest The Rock to his daughter as her running mate, believing that the power of celebrity will give her the White House.

Every single man on this planet wants to create a lasting legacy. They want to be remembered once their time on Earth is done. This is shown most strongly in the concept of nepotism - where parents gift to their children status and power, in order to continue their family name.

Donald Trump is no different. He wants the Trump name to be forever remembered. If his daughter were to also win the White House, he would go down in history as being one of the most influential men to ever lead the United States. After all, the two George Bushs did the exact same thing.

But where does this leave Shawn? Does he believe that a joint Conway / Mendes ticket will take out the White House? Could a Canadian pop singer and a powerful pollster end up leading America?

Shawn is not convinced. He believes that Conway has tarnished herself with the Trump administration and does not have a future in the White House. Once she is eventually sacked by Trump (which she will be, as Ivanka will use her witchery to convince her father to get rid of her rival), she will fall into irrelevancy and no longer be discussed. Just like Bernie Sanders, in the decades to come she will not be remembered, for better or for worse.

Would there be a better Republican candidate for him to team up with, if he does indeed want to run in 2020? Would Arnold Schwarzenegger be an effective running mate? Together, the pop sensation and the Terminator could offer a new age for America. Or perhaps a Republican Senator or Governor would be a better fit?

Shawn is also not happy with these ideas. After all, America showed in 2016 that they are not happy with the establishment. Schwarzenegger, despite his movie background, has become part of the establishment after serving as Governor of California. The Senators and other Governors are also establishment figures. America still wants a fresh approach to governing. Despite some believing that the Trump experiment has gone horribly wrong, they have not given up on the idea of injecting an outsider into Washington to shake things up. This is why there are still some Democrats wanting Sanders to run again in 2020.

This would then lead readers to one conclusion - Shawn Mendes will not be vying for President of the United States in 2020. Many Americans will breathe a sigh of relief that a Canadian will not seek to destroy their country. Or will they?

Michelle Obama has reportedly expressed interest in having Shawn Mendes as her running mate in the next election. Even though Shawn wants the top job, he is apparently prepared to accept the Vice Presidency, if Michelle agrees to hand over power to him in 2028, after serving two terms. Shawn would only be thirty at the time, a young age to be President. But after serving two terms as Vice President,

Americans would begin to view him as a fellow American, rather than as a Canadian invader.

Michelle also has a cunning plan to recruit Kellyann Conway to the Democrats. She will offer her a role as Ambassador to Russia. Whilst some may question this as being a foolish move, Michelle believes that after suffering through the Trump Russian links, the public will want an ambassador that is too honest on Twitter. Given that Conway tweets confidential information, there will be no transparency issues during her tenure.

Conway would be a valuable addition, as she would bring along her polling experience.

In conjunction with this plan, Michelle has asked Shawn to sabotage Trump's wall proposal. This way, James Corden will still be able to get into the country. The secret-President of Mexico will be a thorn in Trump's side which can only help Michelle's campaign. Even if Trump decides not to run in 2020, and Ivanka Trump runs instead, President Corden will seek to undermine anyone with the surname Trump.

And as for Arnold Schwarzenegger? He also despises the Trump family and could be enticed to the Democrats, if the price is right. By 2020, he may realise his presidential ambitions will never come to pass. This does not mean that he cannot secure a key position within the administration. Michelle will offer him the role as Secretary of State, only to infuriate Trump who wants the celebrities on his side.

With Weinstein going to be behind bars, Michelle does not need to fear Hollywood turning on her. Rather, with her influence as the founding member of the AWJL alongside Ellen, she will be able to influence Hollywood to support her. Trump will be left upset that all of the celebrities are endorsing his opponent, which will make him more likely to make a mistake.

Michelle hopes that this will force Trump to reveal that he and Rosie O'Donnell are in a relationship, so he has some celebrity power behind him. This would then result in Melania Trump being deactivated and sent back to Japan to be sold for parts. With the loss of his greatest security personnel, but, more importantly, the loss of having the head of the NRA support him, he will find it difficult to fund a full campaign in 2020.

Whilst all of this may sound like a good plan, Ivanka's witchery is impressive and could sway the election in the Trump family's favour. How will Shawn negate the impact of her witchcraft?

The answer - Donald Trump Junior.

Filled with jealousy about his sister, he could be manipulated into taking away his sister's powers. Everybody knows that witches can only lose their magic if a family member takes away their Halloween candy, and Trump Junior has shown a history of being more than happy to take away candy if it means teaching young children about the perils of socialism.

Trump Junior will destroy his sister's witchery ability, rendering her a normal human and unable to control peoples' minds. The 2020 election will then be on an even footing.

And who would win in this contest between Trump / The Rock and Obama / Mendes? Well, after four years of Donald Trump as President, the public may want a change. They may long for the more classy days of the Obama administration, where tweets were not made at midnight and press secretaries did not dress up as bunnies to frighten small children. Or perhaps they may prefer a strong leader who is not afraid of saying what he thinks. Perhaps they will want another four years of the Trump administration.

Your correspondent believes that 2020 will be an interesting year. It is highly likely that Donald Trump will not contest the election, but will hand the baton to his daughter. And what does your correspondent think the outcome of the election will be? Does your correspondent believe that the master Trump will win, or his apprentice Shawn?

Well...

All hail President Mendes!

Acknowledgements

To Dane at eBook Launch, thank you so much for designing another brilliant cover.

To Kayleigh, my close friend, thank you for all the hours you have spent critiquing my work.

To my grandmother, who spent time looking through this work and no doubt questioned my sanity.

And to my mother, who also spends hours reading my work, thank you.

Thank you to all of my readers at my Facebook page (@JacksonBrownAuthor) who regularly read my work. This is for you.

But above all, thank you to everyone that was mentioned in this book. Please do not sue me.